The Market of the Gods

Business & Innovation

Vol. 36

The creation of new activities, of news production and consumption modes, of new goods and services, of new markets and new jobs (etc.) depends as much on the heroic action of entrepreneurs as on the strategies of big corporations which develop their activities at a global scale. Innovation and business are interlinked. The main themes of the books published in this series are: Entrepreneurship, enterprise and innovation; Innovation strategies in a global context; Innovation policies and business climate; Innovation, business dynamics and socio-economic change. The synergies between innovative entrepreneurship, firms' strategies and innovation policies is of major importance in the explanation of technological paradigms change and of the transformations in economic and social structures of wealthy and less wealthy countries. In this series are published books in English or in French specialized in economics, management and sociology of innovation and also dealing with change and entrepreneurship in a local, national or international perspective.

This series is supported by the Research Network on Innovation.

Series editors :
Dimitri UZUNIDIS, Blandine LAPERCHE, Sophie BOUTILLIER :
Université du Littoral (France), Seattle University (USA) et
Wesford Business School (Lyon, Genève, France, Switzerland),
Research Network on Innovation.
Viktor PROKOP: University of Pardubice, Czech Republic, Research
Network on Innovation.

Dominique Desjeux

The Market of the Gods
How religious innovations emerge
From Judaism to Christianity

PETER LANG

Bruxelles - Berlin - Chennai - Lausanne - New York - Oxford

Library of Congress Cataloging-in-Publication Data
A CIP catalog record for this book has been applied for at the Library of Congress.

Bibliographic Information published by the Deutsche Nationalbibliothek
The Deutsche Nationalbibliothek lists this publication in the Deutsche Nationalbibliografie; detailed bibliographic data is available online at http://dnb.d-nb.de.

The book was translated by Suzanne Kobine-Roy.
French edition: Dominique Desjeux, Le marché des dieux, PUF, 2022.
ISBN 978-2-13-083601 © Presses Universitaires de France/Humensis, 2022.

ISBN 978-3-0343-5003-7 • ISSN 2034-5402
E-ISBN 978-3-0343-5004-4 (ePDF) • E-ISBN 978-3-0343-5005-1 (ePUB)
DOI 10.3726/b22071 D/2024/5678/33

2024 Peter Lang Group AG, Lausanne
Published by Peter Lang Éditions Scientifiques Internationales - P.I.E., Brussels, Belgium

info@peterlang.com - www.peterlang.com

All rights reserved.

All parts of this publication are protected by copyright. Any utilisation outside the strict limits of the copyright law, without the permission of the publisher, is forbidden and liable to prosecution. This applies in particular to reproductions, translations, microfilming, and storage and processing in electronic retrieval systems.

This publication has been peer-reviewed.

By the Same Author

The anthropological perspective of the world. The inductive method illustrated, Peter Lang, 2018.

Consommations émergentes. La fin d'une société de consommation?, with P. Moati (dir.), Le Bord de l'eau, 2016.

Les méthodes qualitatives, with S. Alami and I. Garabuau-Moussaoui, Puf, "Que-sais-je?", 2009, 4th edition, 2024.

La consommation, Puf, "Que-sais-je?" 2006.

Les sciences sociales, Puf, "Que-sais-je?" 2004.

Comment les Chinois voient les Européens, with L. Zheng and A-S. Boisard, Puf, 2003.

L'édition en sciences humaines, with I. Orhant and S. Taponier, L'Harmattan, 1991.

Le sens de l'autre. Stratégies, réseaux et cultures en situation interculturelle, with S. Taponier, L'Harmattan, 1991.

Le système d'intervention de l'État en matière industrielle et ses relations avec le milieu industriel, with E. Friedberg, AUDIR, Micro-Hachette, 1973.

Contents

By the Same Author 7

Introduction 11

Chapter 1 The Anthropology of Innovation Applied to
Religious Phenomena 15

Chapter 2 Mesopotamia, the Matrix of Jewish Monotheism in
a Polytheistic World (12th to 5th Centuries BC) 25

Chapter 3 The Hellenization and Romanization of the
Mediterranean Rim 39

Chapter 4 Two Great Debates in the Jewish
World: Circumcision and Proselytism 47

Chapter 5 The Incremental Invention Launched by
Jesus: Purifying the Temple Religion 57

Chapter 6 Paul the Apostle on the Road to Disruptive
Innovation 71

Chapter 7 The Destruction of the Temple: The Incremental
Invention Becomes a Disruptive Innovation 87

Chapter 8 The Struggle Between Rabbinic Judaism and Christianity for Control of the Synagogues 99

Chapter 9 How the Instability of the Roman Empire Favoured the Christian Innovation 111

Conclusion 125
Postscript 129
Notes 139
Bibliography 155

Introduction

Nor do they put new wine into old wineskins, or else the wineskins break, the wine is spilled, and the wineskins are ruined. But they put new wine into new wineskins, and both are preserved.

(Gospel according to Matthew 9:17[1])

Andrianampoinimerina was a great Malagasy king who ruled the Kingdom of Imerina from 1787 to 1810. He once declared that he had "only one friend, rice [...] I build dykes to ensure there is water for your rice paddies[2]". He organized and united his kingdom in the highlands of Madagascar by creating a centralized irrigation system with water police to ensure everyone had access to it, and a tax system, called the *hetra* in Malagasy, which "represented the size of a rice paddy required to feed a family [or around 0.8 hectares]. It served as the tax base and was also used for census-taking". He retained agrarian rituals linked to venerating ancestors (*famadihana*, or the turning of the bones[3]), such as "the ceremonial sacrifice of oxen as an offering to the 'land owner' before developing an untouched valley" and tavy, bushfires started before the rainy season to purify the soil and regenerate pasture lands on the hillsides[4].

All the components were there, everything that makes a society and determines its survival and development: land, rice, water, seasons, family farmers, political authority, military conquests and the supernatural dimension with ancestor worship. Even if this great king did not invent the dyke, he was its "mobilizing figure", like Paul the Apostle for Christianity, Lenin for the soviet revolution or Steve Jobs for the smartphone. These innovative hydraulic systems predated his reign, but it was he who organized their widespread dissemination across a large part of Madagascar's highland plateaus.

I first encountered Madagascar's paddy fields in 1972, falling in love with this beautiful plant that begins as a soft green seedling and turns a bright golden colour by harvest time. I was doing research for an agricultural development project, the GOPR (*Groupement Opération Productivité Rizicole*), seeking to understand what makes farmers accept or reject new technology when it is offered to them.

The GOPR's objective was to disseminate a range of agricultural technologies among farmers. This included applying fertilizer (nitrates, phosphates and potash) and planting rice in rows rather than randomly so as to facilitate the introduction of further technology, rotary tillers. They are much more effective for controlling weeds in straight-planted rice paddies, meaning the rice faces less competition for nutrients from weeds. These are unsophisticated, low-tech innovations that rely on male physical energy and should therefore be adopted without any real problems. They are relatively simple to use and promise to significantly increase rice yields and thereby family farmers' income.

Contrary to everything the agronomists expected, female employees in the agriculture sector were against adopting rotary tillers. The technicians put this economically and technically "irrational" attitude down to the fact that the women were supposedly "traditional" in their behaviours, rather like the "dormitive principle of opium" in *The Imaginary Invalid*. For Molière, who is mocking physicians, this "virtue" explains little. It is neither true nor false. It cannot be proved.

In reality, the women's resistance to the innovation was entirely rational: this new weeding technique had to be performed by men. Rotary tillers would replace women's work and the salary they received for weeding by hand. This new technology would mean the loss of a large share of their annual income, and so they opposed it in what proved ultimately to be an unsuccessful effort to avert a fall in income.

After working on innovation processes in agriculture, business, mass retail, public administration and in the home in numerous countries, I began working on a new study in 2019. I wanted to understand how the birth of Christianity came about and more importantly, what caused it to spread throughout the Greco-Roman world.

An anthropological reading of society, human relationships and beliefs is not inherently more true than other interpretations. Delphine Horvilleur is a rabbi who tells the well-known story by Hungarian rabbi Reb Shlomo, which ends like this:

The learned student crosses the plains of Russia on horseback and finally reaches Reb Shlomo, who is on his deathbed but is, thanks be to God, still alive. With some difficulty, he opens his eyes and recognizes his student. The student says: "Reb Shlomo, I went to see Moïshe to tell him what you said." You told us: "life is an arrow". He said: "life is not an arrow". With his dying breath, old Reb Shlomo replies: "Yes, you could put it that way too".

What Delphine Horvilleur means is that "there are always several ways to tell the story, several ways to tell the truth [...] interpretation tells us that it is never the sole pronouncement of meaning or of truth[5]". This story confirms that multiple interpretations are possible.

Anthropology provides a methodological contribution, in that it helps us change the focal point of our observation of change in society[6],. It helps extract us from the "cognitive tunnels" that restrict our exploration of reality, while accumulating mobile knowledge, thereby opening up a diversity of causes and worlds. Anthropology is critical in that it discusses possible analyses but without condemning or "enchanting" them, since social reality is an ambivalent space where "good" and "bad" are intertwined and inseparable. Anthropology invites us to take a different look at human behaviours so as to take different action. It practices observation. It describes the ambivalence in society before passing judgement. It prefers understanding before outrage. It is therefore a comprehensive approach. It does not seek to justify any situation in society. It looks at the how before the why, because the explanation lies in the combination of constraints the actors face. It seeks to decipher the logic behind the "irrational".

This is why anthropology is not only cultural. It is also strategic. In this study, I observe the power games and the social network effects behind the emergence of Jewish and Christian monotheism in a predominantly polytheistic world. The explanatory model used in this book is summed up by the term "strategic anthropology".

We use the interplay of actors' behaviours to analyze social logic that appears technically, economically or theologically irrational. Human or social rationales are not the same as in life sciences or natural science. Social logic disrupts the biological, technical and economic logics within which it is nonetheless embedded. It is also very different from the logics of religion or faith.

Anthropology shows that some elements of human behaviours are permanent but that, at the same time, everything is always changing.

Although there are occasional peaceful periods, everything is in conflict, as origin myths have always told us. Take Cronos, who used a sickle to castrate his father Uranus, the husband of Gaia, and ate his own offspring lest one of them overthrow him[7]. This is why anthropology seeks neither to condemn nor enchant Zoroastrianism, Judaism, Christianity or paganism, which each carry their share of domination and liberation.

Chapter 1

The Anthropology of Innovation Applied to Religious Phenomena

Between 1965 and 1967, I studied exegesis under Father Tamisier. Later on and rather unexpectedly, this critical training would lead me to an agnostic approach towards religions and towards the world, as neither an atheist nor a believer but with understanding towards the diversity of approaches[1]. The divine causality, which is a matter of religious faith, is set to one side.

Tracking the Emergence of Christianity: Wrong Turns and False Starts

The "maps" that I had to explore this new territory were sketchy at best. The history of Christianity and Judaism had greatly evolved since the 1990s[2], and I began my research with no clear view of where I would end up. My main tool was the anthropological "compass" I had cobbled together as I carried out or oversaw dozens of studies of innovation processes in the modern world.

It helps me to navigate whenever I venture into fields in which I am not a specialist, fields that are like exotic worlds for me, such as the digital sector, Chinese families, sorcery in the Congo or beauty in Brazil. To get my bearings, I observe the puzzle piece by piece, finding markers in everyday practices, the role of logistics, material culture and social networks, the interplay between actors and the strategic function of the magical and religious practices that organize every society and thereby every social phenomenon.

For this research, the milestones would gradually emerge from historico-religious sources that were often incomplete on many points but always extremely thorough. They were all written by Catholic, Protestant, Jewish or agnostic researchers and are impressive works of erudition from translations of ancient languages. I am grateful to these researchers for the days and no doubt nights they spent deciphering often illegible texts so that we may access them. The tremendous work done by these researchers, who are often unknown beyond their field, was a humbling place for me to begin this anthropological study.

Fragment by fragment, I followed the traces of the emergence of Christianity. Initially I set out to show how Paul the Apostle had been a good strategist in that he understood that the "Christian" innovation would never take in the Greco-Roman world unless it did away with circumcision and kashrut, both precepts that came from Judaism.

I had already observed that an innovation would only spread beyond its context of origin if it was reinterpreted and transformed by its new setting. This is why here, I will frequently draw comparisons between past centuries and today's world. Contemporary examples demonstrate the continuity of human behaviours through the centuries and can also provide more-vivid illustrations when the past can seem obscure[3].

Another advantage of drawing comparisons, even seemingly shocking ones, is to show how what seems abnormal today already existed in the past, just in a different form. If we can grasp this continuity, then when disaster strikes our society—be it a pandemic or a climate crisis—the problems seem more familiar and we are better equipped to act.

One example that comes to mind, far removed from religion but that mobilizes similar social mechanisms, is that of cognac in China. In France, it is customary to drink cognac after dinner. In China, one of the reasons it is so successful is that it has been reinterpreted to be served like Moutai, a strong clear spirit made from sorghum and used for the many toasts to friends, co-workers and clients throughout the entire meal[4].

This relatively mundane illustration exemplifies what occurred in the fourth century AD between Christianity and polytheism. In order to develop, Christianity had to reinterpret some pagan practices by incorporating them into Christian rituals. The anthropological mechanism of reinterpretation, translation[5] or hybridization[6] of inventions is an invariable in innovation processes.

Paganism as Both Source and Receiver of Monotheism

As my research progressed, I understood that we cannot really talk about Christians in the first century AD and that I was on the wrong track in my efforts to understand the shift from invention to innovation, i.e. the spread of Christianity as a social process that led to the religious novelty being received. Rather, the innovation I needed to focus on was not so much the origin of Christianity but of "oriental" monotheism, and more specifically from the "fertile crescent" from the Nile to the Tigris and Euphrates, from where Jewish and then Christian monotheism emerged, albeit not in a linear fashion. I then realized that it would be difficult to solve the mystery of the origins of monotheism because there was no pure, single, visible start to this invention. Like most innovation processes, there is no clear-cut start or finish.

There was another mystery hidden in the invention of monotheism: the mystery of how it spread throughout a polytheistic Greco-Roman world that was completely hostile to it. Until the fourth century AD, the dominant political and magico-religious circles of the western and northern Mediterranean believed in multiple deities. Martin P. Nilsson cites an author who says *"somewhat exaggeratedly that the Gods outnumbered the men*[7]*"*. Beliefs to the east and south were more ambivalent. Here, monotheism was already emerging in Egypt, along the east coast of the Mediterranean in the Levant, and in Mesopotamia.

I discovered that in a polytheistic agrarian civilization, adopting monotheism represented a significant risk to food security and human health. This, as I will show below, was the case in the Jewish world between the sixth century BC, after the Jewish elite returned from the Babylonian captivity, and the first century BC, at the time of the construction of the Second Temple of Jerusalem. This obstacle to the reception of monotheism should have been insurmountable.

In some ways, monotheism should never have succeeded beyond its initial era of influence because it excluded other religions, unlike polytheism which is inclusive, which does not mean non-violent. Rather than exclude, polytheism looks for equivalences with existing divinities[8]. It looks for things that are comparable and includes them in the world of its own deities[9]. With the Hellenization of Palestine in the fourth century BC, Greek polytheism began to strongly influence Jewish culture, as we will see later with the matter of circumcision. Jewish monotheism felt that it was under threat from Hellenization. Later on, it would be polytheism's turn to feel threatened. As I investigated, I discovered that around the first century AD, at the time of Jesus, Judaism was expanding and gaining significant ground across the Greco-Roman world from Mesopotamia to Italy. Between 6 % and 8 % of the population of the Roman Empire were Jewish. In my investigations into Jewish and Christian monotheistic innovation in a polytheistic world, I came to understand as much about the "Christian Jewish" invention as about the difficulties of it being received into a Greco-Roman world that perceived monotheism as superstitious atheism, an irrational religion and a threat to the community[10].

Jewish and then Christian monotheism are therefore analyzed as "inventions" that became innovations. This distinction is the foundation of Norbert Alter's interpretive model on innovations, itself inspired by Schumpeter. With the hindsight of history, it is clear that Jesus' objective was more to create "incremental innovation" designed to clear the dead wood out of the Jewish religion than "disruptive innovation"[11] in the form of a new religion.

This places us at the heart of the enigma posed by all innovation processes: what is it that allows an innovation to develop successfully in a context that it disrupts so strongly? How much continuity and discontinuity is there between the invention in its original context and its reception into a new one[12]? How much of its adoption is forced and how much is voluntary or by imitation? And when it succeeds, who wins and who loses? Ultimately, in the Gospel according to Matthew, Jesus states that he has not come to abolish the Law of Moses but to accomplish its purpose (Matt. 5:17). He positions himself in continuity with Judaism. This is why new wine is in fact often stored in old wineskins.

The meeting of two worlds that occurs in innovation processes is rarely fluid. Most of the time, these processes involve conflict and end with winners and losers.

The Importance of Systemic Crises

My investigation, worthy of a crime novel, shows that all throughout history, as monotheistic innovation spread, it took advantage of multiple military, monetary, economic and even climate crises to infiltrate a world that was hostile to it.

The Babylonian captivity in the sixth century BC[13] placed part of the Jewish populations of the northern Kingdom of Israel and the southern Kingdom of Judah in contact with Mesopotamian "monotheism". The Jews—or Judeans when referring to the region around Jerusalem—already believed in Yahweh but had not abandoned their old agrarian deities. According to historian Mario Liverani, Yahweh likely came from the south, and religious historian Nissim Amzallag confirms Yahweh's southern origins, linked to a crisis in the copper economy in the twelfth century BC.

Another crisis, political and military this time, is the Maccabean Revolt in the second century BC, when the idea of resurrection emerged in Judaism, something the Christian movement would lean on heavily.

The most decisive crisis was triggered by the destruction of the Second Temple in 70 AD. This opened the way for competition between different factions of Judaism from which Christianity would emerge.

The period of global warming, which began in the second century BC and ended 400 years later as the Roman Empire entered the Crisis of the Third Century, was followed by a monetary crisis in the following century. It heralded the end of paganism's monopoly and created a key strategic opening for Christian development.

Crises open windows of opportunity for innovations to rush through. But Christianity's success did not come down to crises alone. There was also a "horizon of expectation[14]" for "Greek monotheism", which tended to be reserved for the elite[15]. The fourth-century-AD Emperor Constantine appears to have been sympathetic to the idea. He "like his ancestors, worshipped the Sun God; he probably confused the god Chrestos, that so many people spoke so highly of, with this single God referred to by more or less all the religions at the time[16]".

By the fourth century AD, when my investigation ends, the Greco-Roman polytheism of the elite was already steeped in monotheism[17]. This monotheism would serve as a "toothing stone" to which Christian monotheism could attach itself[18].

Christianity Re-Appropriates Some Pagan Practices

Christianity's success is also linked to the reinterpretation of some pagan practices, as shown by the historian Ramsay MacMullen:

The pagan system had a very different structure which events forced upon the church and so in good measure re-shaped it [...] It requires, however, the defining of religion as something more than a creed; it requires a definition more in the style of pagans, or of anthropologists (though of the ancient bishops, too), rather than in the style of yesterday's historian[19].

Ramsay MacMullen suggests that the anthropological approach to rituals, which is an agnostic one[20], can be helpful in understanding the process of religious innovation. Above all, he confirms that storing new wine can require old wineskins. Innovation is always comprised of continuity and discontinuity. This is its central paradox.

Some inventions become innovations, meaning that they go through a process of organization that transforms them and renders them acceptable in their environment. They then enter the collective customs of a society or a group when a systemic crisis transforms an old configuration into a new one. During the shift to a new and unstable equilibrium, everything is blurred, making it difficult to attribute the origin to a single cause.

This is happening today with the combination of the war in Ukraine, the COVID-19 pandemic, the climate crisis, a surge in populism, the geopolitical shift caused by the rise of China and Asia, and the economic crisis hitting not only the transport sector but also all services that rely on mobility, such as live entertainment or restaurants, all combined with the unexpected boom in remote working and e-commerce. We are dealing with a systemic crisis, the consequences of which remain uncertain and will emerge progressively as societies evolve.

Today, there are only unknowns. Unknowns generate fear, which in turn "creates an intense need for explanation [...]. Explanation is the antidote to anxiety[21]". Yet these explanations can be taken from science or equally from ill-defined magical and religious practices. The latter reappear throughout the ages under different labels: "witchcraft", "superstition", "conspiracy theories" or even "cognitive bias". The fact that the magico-religious is hypercoherent makes it irrefutable, which is why it is so useful in the face of anxiety and also so limited compared to what is true. Science can be refuted because it seeks what is true and not the truth, because it has flaws and is open to dispute. It is its fragility that makes it strong and meaningful.

Conclusion: The Shift From Polytheism to Monotheism Between the Fourth Century BC and the Fourth Century AD

Our journey will span several centuries and take us down some unexpected paths, with some surprising stops along the way, helping us understand the early forms of globalization and the spread of innovation via religion.

Our investigation begins with the copper crisis at the end of the Mycenaean civilization in the Aegean, around the twelfth century BC. This crisis helped the emergence of "Yahweh", who was the God of blacksmiths in the mountains south of the Dead Sea. The Jews adopted Yahweh in the eleventh century BC when King David created the southern Kingdom of Judah. In the tenth century BC, King Solomon dedicated a temple to Yahweh in Jerusalem, one that would later be destroyed by the Babylonian Empire that lasted from the eighth to the seventh century BC. The ensuing exile in Babylon on the banks of the Euphrates in the sixth century BC bolstered the monotheist movement and influenced the Genesis narrative in the Jewish Torah.

The second turning point came with the Greek Empire of Alexander the Great, lasting from the fourth to the second century BC. During this era, Israel was exposed to polytheism, which was associated with Hellenistic modernity and attracted part of the Jewish elite.

Then came the Roman Empire, which lasted from the first century BC to the fifth century AD. That empire destroyed the Second Temple of Jerusalem in 70 AD, providing monotheistic Christian Jews with an opportunity to expand and split from their Jewish origins. In the fourth century AD, paganism ceased to be the sole state religion and when that monopoly ended, Christianity was free to spread.

The novel idea—the invention of monotheism—embedded itself into the religious, cultural and political diversity of the Mediterranean world, which was more receptive to monotheism in the East and to polytheism in the West. This diversity would evolve over eight centuries between the fourth century BC with Alexander the Great (356–323 BC) and the fourth century AD of Constantine the Great (272–337).

When Christianity became an institution in the fourth century AD, it broke partially from Roman paganism and rabbinic Judaism but did not reject everything. The Greek, Jewish and Roman cultures formed the matrix from which Christianity emerged and into which it was received.

My investigation mainly covers these eight centuries, and particularly between the second century BC and the rise of the Jewish diaspora all around the Mediterranean and the second century AD, when a dissident Jewish current emerged that would become Christianity in the West and East.

Nonetheless, my objective remains an anthropological one: to seek out invariants, the universal mechanisms of innovation processes beyond their historical variabilities, so as to demonstrate how they can shed light on innovation processes in societies, organizations or families today. As an anthropologist, I select the characteristics that are common to other innovation processes in order to work towards a more general abstract model. I only retain that which does not vary and which constitutes a stable structure, and then I reintroduce the diversity of the types of changes.

Like the polytheistic religions, I look for equivalences between past and present events. Systemic crises are not the sole preserve of the financial sector, despite how things may have looked in 2008. In the past and today, they continue to function as events that trigger change and innovations, even if their exact content remains unpredictable. Logistics, energy, material objects, climate, disease, languages, the interplay between actors, social imaginaries, are all constantly recombining to produce something new, be it positive or negative. Geography is crucial to our ability to understand the host of situations that led to the emergence of Jewish and Christian monotheism. It was the rivers, coastlines and mountains that determined how territories were conquered and ideas spread, based on the circulation of humans and the animals that carried them.

One recent equivalent of this today is the success of the application Zoom as a result of the COVID-19 pandemic. Zoom went from 10 million users at the end of 2019 to 200 million in 2020, going from video-conferencing start-up to a competitor of the largest global operators.

In the mid-first century, the group of Christian Jews following Jesus, who could be compared to a *start-up*, numbered no more than a few thousand out of an imperial population of 70 million. Two hundred and fifty years later, there were nearly 9 million Christians of Jewish origin.

Conclusion

This shift from invisible invention to collective innovation is the central mystery to be solved.

In order to work, the comparative method used must be "neo-nominalist", to refer to the fourteenth-century William of Ockham, i.e. words should be taken as a means to describe a reality based on the combined views of actors and observers, and not as a stable essence defined by timeless external actors or by a dictionary. One word, such as monotheism, can describe several realities, and several words, such as pagan, gentile and polytheist, can describe the same reality. Words have no value per se. They do not refer to a hidden essence. Their meaning depends on the context in which they are used. What I am saying here is of course controversial. Each researcher observes the past from a different angle, hence the comparative method can be problematic when it comes to interpreting the past.

There are many problems when it comes to reconstituting monotheism's innovation process, including the confusion among the terms that various intellectual branches use to describe it. As the philosopher and anthropologist Maurizio Bettini points out, "the terms 'polytheism', 'paganism' and 'idolatry' were all coined from the perspective of a single God[22]". They are often pejorative. Today, the most neutral or least connoted ones are polytheism and ancient religion.

We must remember that the Romans viewed Judaism and Christianity as superstitions, while considering themselves to be pious and venerating of their gods[23].

The meaning of all these terms only stabilizes once one side has beaten the other. All of this can continue to evolve over time but it cannot be expunged from the past, contrary to cancel culture's tenet that the past can be erased when it is deemed to be negative. There are already examples of this in the Stalinist regime, where photographs of Soviet politicians disappeared with the rise or fall of each political current.

The problem is the same for the use of terms such as Palestine, Israel or Judea. They correspond to variations in the Jewish kingdom. The term Palestine was used by the Greek historian Herodotus in the fifth century BC[24]. Depending on the sources, references to Israel or Jewish Palestine can mean Judea in the south (around Jerusalem and inhabited by Judeans), Galilee in the north and Samaria in the centre (the modern West Bank). Describing Jews or Hebrews as a homogeneous whole does not make much historical sense. The Jewish population, like all populations in the world, is heterogeneous, including when it comes to doctrine (from "liberal" to "orthodox").

For example, the Samaritans only recognize the Pentateuch (penta, πέντε five in Greek) as holy scripture. These five books, beginning with Genesis, form the Hebrew Torah and the start of the Old Testament in the Christian Bible (*byblos*, from Βύβλος = papyrus, which became βίβλος = book in ancient Greek). The Pentateuch does not include the oral commentary that was written down in the first century AD by what became known as "rabbinic Judaism", after the destruction of the Second Temple of Jerusalem in 70 AD.

This commentary was written into Jewish tradition in the Mishnah and then later on in the Talmud around the fifth century AD. Thus the content of Jewish monotheism is also heterogeneous and, like all religious phenomena, a matter of controversy. All these terms, be they of Roman, Greek, Jewish or Christian origin, are used in this book for convenience only, or because they were used by the authors in their various publications[25].

Observation is at the heart of this inductive method, which does not look for frequencies, correlations or series, but rather for invariable human mechanisms that are mobilized in various ways depending on the interplay of actors. In other words, the why emerges from the how. The how is born from patient description, which I am well aware is always imperfect, but to me, what matters is not perfection but rigour in the way a study progresses.

~ ~ ~

Chapter 2

Mesopotamia, the Matrix of Jewish Monotheism in a Polytheistic World (12th to 5th Centuries BC)

Irrespective of the terms used to describe the different religions, Jewish monotheism seems to have been born at the same time as the Kingdom of Israel in the eleventh century BC. Thus, the historic development of monotheism is connected to military power and territorial conquests. It did not develop overnight. There was a long and tense cohabitation between polytheism and monotheism in Judaism that lasted at least until the destruction of the Second Temple in 70 AD and probably longer.

The Temple's destruction led to the disappearance of ritual sacrifices that were not that different from Greco-Roman pagan practices, as confirmed by this quotation from religious historian Martin Nilsson: "Animal sacrifice was the core ritual of the Greek religion. The parts of the sacrificed animal that belonged to the Gods were burned on the altar, and those participating in the sacrifice roasted their share on the same fire[1]." For the priests of the Temple of Jerusalem, this same ritual was also a core practice. Two beliefs—such as monotheism and polytheism—can appear very distinct when viewed from a distance in the rear-view mirror of history, when in fact the boundary between them is often blurry when viewed close up.

Between Moses in the Sinai and Cain's Descendents, the Blacksmiths in the Negev

For certain authors, the Kingdom of Israel began in the eleventh century BC when King David had himself "proclaimed first King of Judah (in the south) and then King of Judah and Israel (in the north). He made Jerusalem the capital. It was the year 1000[2]". The kingdom is said to have stretched from south of the Dead Sea to the Euphrates in northern Syria and incorporated vassal kingdoms[3]. Historian Mario Liverani believes that the kingdom was narrower than this, stretching from Galilee in the North to the semi-arid zones of the southern Negev minus part of the coastline held by the Philistines[4]. King David's son King Solomon (c. 970–931 BC) built the First Temple in Jerusalem at what is said to have been the height of the Kingdom of Israel. For other authors, such as the archaeologist Israel Finkelstein and the biblical scholar Thomas Römer, the Kingdom of David in the south was very small compared to its competitor, the Kingdom of Israel to the north[5]. Historically then, the great king would therefore be neither David nor Solomon but Jeroboam II, whose northern kingdom disappeared in 720 BC. The Hebrews were still hesitating between polytheism and monotheism.

Both in history and in legend, Jewish monotheism has multiple origins. First, there is the official but disputed origin in the Sinai desert where, according to Exodus, the second book of the Pentateuch in both the Jewish Torah and the Christian Old Testament, Yahweh, God, appeared to Moses and delivered the Ten Commandments. We know nothing historically about Moses, only that he did not reach the Promised Land of Canaan, "Palestine" i.e. the "land of the Philistines[6]". Whether the event itself is legend or historical fact, he died before and so probably in the eleventh century BC. Part of the Pentateuch, which is attributed to Moses, appears to have been inspired by Babylonian culture, which the Jewish elite discovered during their exile in the Assyrian capital five hundred years later, in the sixth century BC. The oldest written texts in the Torah date back to the end of the eighth century BC and this Babylonian period. The creation narrative and the story of Noah both appear to have been inspired by this culture.

In 2021, the biologist and religious historian Nissim Amzallag proposed an additional origin of Jewish monotheism. In a book that reads like a detective story or a "whodunit[7]", he shows how the cult of Yahweh (YHWH), the God of Israel, originally came from a mining region in the Arava desert that stretched the length of the Negev from north to south between the Dead Sea and the Gulf of Aqaba (between modern Beersheba and Eilat)[8]. This area was inhabited by the Kenites, who were the descendants of Cain, "an instructer of every artificer in brass and iron" according to Genesis 4:22. At the start of the second millennium BC, ten centuries before Israel was created, the Kenites were metalworkers and more specifically coppersmiths. Their output was later supplanted by the copper production of Cyprus in the Mediterranean. Thus, Cain was a positive character.

Control over copper mines has always been a geopolitical issue, in the past to produce weapons from copper alloy and today for the copper wiring that makes electricity and digital activity possible. Between the 15th and 12th centuries BC, "there was a sharp decline in copper production in Cyprus". This coincided with the weakening of Egypt and the collapse of the great kingdoms of Anatolia (the Hittites, in modern Turkey), Mesopotamia (modern Iraq) and the Aegean Sea (the Mycenaean civilization, in modern Greece). These great kingdoms collapsed as a result of a "period of drought in the late 14th century that caused severe agricultural crises and famines". This led to a period "of wars, social upheaval and migration[9]". Moreover, copper distribution networks were vulnerable to pirates, and to top it all, a plague epidemic appears to have struck the Mediterranean and Middle East in the fifteenth century BC.

The crisis in the Mediterranean copper economy supported a revival of metalworking in the Negev, in the south of Israel. The copper mines of Faynan in the northern Negev and Timna in the south were booming between the twelfth and the ninth century BC. This narrowly preceded and probably contributed to the unification of the Kingdom of Israel, either by King David, or later after the northern Kingdom of Israel disappeared.

The health, climate, military, political and logistical crises in the twelfth century BC[10], which Eric H. Cline describes as a "systemic collapse", created a window of opportunity for the metalworkers of the Negev in southern Judea. They proved to be a stroke of good fortune for them and for their deity Yahweh, the god of the forge. He was the equivalent of Vulcan, who gave us the word *volcano* and was the Roman god of fire and hence of metalworking, and of Hephaestus for the Greeks: "How, in these circumstances, could the god and patron of metalworking not become the hero of the liberation of the Southern Levant and the renaissance of nations?[11]". Yahweh symbolized the Kenite's economic success and liberation from Egyptian domination. The power attributed to Yahweh was proportionate to the coppersmiths' new economic power.

The Hebrews went on to adopt the Kenite's Yahweh and change its status from deity of a group of metalworkers to deity of an entire people. This reinterpretation required Yahweh's Kenite origins to disappear, and so they were denigrated. The Kenites' ancestor Cain became the murderer of his brother Abel and the unsavoury character immortalized by Victor Hugo in *La Légende des siècles*: "The eye was in the tomb and fixed on Cain."

It is worth nothing that from the second century AD onwards, the Christians adopted this same mechanism of expunging the Jewish origins of Christianity. This expunging of origins by the receiving community is a mechanism that legitimizes a thriving innovation by "purifying" its provenance.

Between Zoroastrianism, the Babylon Narratives and the Torah

More generally, the belief in a single God and creator is more of an "oriental" invention and can be traced back to Zoroastrianism and to the Gathas, which are attributed to Zarathushtra and addressed to the god Mazda. Conversely, the Egyptians were more polytheistic, like most countries in the western Mediterranean. This does not mean that there is no creation narrative in Greek mythology, quite the contrary: the goddess Gaia, the earth, bears Uranus, the sky, and Pontus, the sea. In a way, geographically, Israel was at the junction of the polytheistic and monotheistic worlds and thus influenced by both.

The Gathas are thought to have been written in Persia (modern Iran) around 1700 BC, although the possible dates range from 3000 to 600 BC according to Khosro Khazai. He writes that on 24 October 1976, the Archbishop of Vienna, Franz König, demonstrated "the Bible's debt to Zarathushtra" and how Zoroastrianism had influenced Christianity via Judaism: "Whoever wishes to understand Jesus must start with the spiritual universe of Zoroastrianism". He points to a filiation between Zoroastrian, Jewish and Christian monotheisms, but this is far from linear and involves much to-ing and fro-ing with polytheism. This is why I talk about a matrix, which is a flexible term that accounts for the interplay between the forces that govern us and humans' room for manoeuvre.

The Jewish elite's exile to Babylon in the sixth century BC could therefore be one of the filiations of monotheism. It was this exile that brought Jewish clergy into much closer contact with Babylonian culture. This influence is probably even older and can be found in several passages of Genesis.

In the Gathas, Zarathushtra describes the creation of the world as follows: "Who has created the earth, sun, moon and stars? [...] Who put the Earth below and *the boundless sky above it*? And who created the water and the verdant nature? [...] Which artist *created lightness and darkness*? [...] O Mazda, tell me, for whom have You created this potent and joyous world?[12]". This text is partially present in Genesis, the Torah's creation narrative: "God saw that the light was good, and God separated the *light from the darkness*. [...] God made the expanse, and it separated the water which was below the expanse from the water which was above the expanse. And it was so. God called *the expanse Sky* [...] Let there be *lights* in the expanse of the sky to separate *day from night*[13]" (Gen. 1:1–26, emphasis by the author).

Similarly, the Mesopotamian Epic of Gilgamesh, thought to date back to around 2000 BC, tells the story of a flood and a god who instructs the king's son to build a boat, that should be roofed over and with a beam equal to her length, then take aboard a pair of all living creatures[14]. This account also inspired the story of the flood and of Noah's ark in Genesis: "And of all that lives, of all flesh, you shall take two of each into the ark to keep alive with you[15]" (Gen. 6:19).

The third Babylonian creation myth that influenced the book of Genesis is called *Enūma eliš* (*the Epic of Creation*)[16]. However, according to Jean Bottéro, one of the leading experts in this era, there is significant discontinuity between the Babylonian narratives and Genesis[17]. The Babylonian myth describes numerous battles among the gods, making it closer to Greek polytheism and the gods of Mount Olympus, who were regularly in conflict.

The Babylonian Captivity was a turning point in the religious thinking of the Jewish people, who reinterpreted the Mesopotamian texts with a more monotheistic slant, perhaps associated with the metalworking Kenites' Yahweh. This emergence of monotheism seems to coincide with the expansion of the Jewish diaspora around the Mediterranean in approximately the fourth century BC, and particularly in Alexandria and Babylon. This diaspora would play a key strategic role in the development of Judaism and then later Christianity. The diaspora can in fact be understood as a "pre-digital" social network, to distinguish it from today's online social networks. It allowed the invention to circulate and be transformed into innovation. There is no innovation without a social network and it was this diaspora that spread monotheism.

The important point to remember is that all these groups—Jews/Hebrews, Galileans, Samaritans or Judeans—whether they remained in Israel, returned from exile in circa the sixth century BC, or even those of them who stayed in Mesopotamia, progressively became monotheistic but were still close to and influenced by the polytheistic world.

The Hebrews Between Polytheism and Monotheism

Certain biblical narratives reprise the Jewish oral traditions dating back to Kings David and Solomon (tenth to ninth century BC), some of which may have already been written down. The Bible's initial books are thought to have been written after the Babylonian Captivity, so several hundred years after the birth of the Kingdom of Israel. As such, they would have been reinterpreted to suit the debates prevailing at the time they were written.

To use a specialist term, the Babylonian culture was probably "henotheistic", meaning polytheistic but with one dominant god, perhaps Yahweh for the Hebrews and Mazda for the Zoroastrians. All of this is up for discussion. However, the term "henotheism" is a good analyzer of the blurred boundaries between monotheism and polytheism, at least between the 10th and 4th centuries BC. As Jean Soler reminds us, the Jews were not always monotheists[18]. Their transition to monotheism was neither conflict- nor pain-free, nor was it linear, as described in the book of Exodus in the Pentateuch (the Torah).

These tensions between polytheism and monotheism appear in the oral traditions of the Jewish people. During the Exodus in the Sinai desert, after they left Egypt possibly around the twelfth or eleventh century BC, while Moses was on Mount Sinai receiving the Ten Commandments as a revelation from God, the Hebrews resorted to worshipping an idol, a golden calf. The context of Moses' encounter with God on the mountain evokes a forge or a volcano. The mountain "was completely in smoke, because the Lord descended upon it in fire. Its smoke ascended like the smoke of a furnace, and the whole mountain quaked greatly[19]". This description appears to connect to Yahweh, the god of the Kenite metalworkers, closer to polytheism than to monotheism.

God spoke to Moses from amidst these clouds of smoke: God spoke all these words, saying: "I am your God who brought you out of the land of Egypt, the house of bondage. You shall have no other gods besides Me.

You shall not make for yourself a sculptured image, or any likeness of what is in the heavens above, or on the earth below, or in the waters under the earth.[20]" [Ex. 20,1–4]

When Moses returned and discovered the Hebrews worshipping an idol, he destroyed it in anger (Ex. 32:1–35). Whether it is real or symbolic, this story is indicative of the tension between monotheism and polytheism among the people of Israel. The Hebrews were not ready to surrender their polytheism without resistance, and for good strategic reasons linked to their agrarian system.

The Links Between Agrarian Ecosystems, Political Systems and Religious Beliefs

Agrarian economies, food security, religious systems and power structures are intimately linked, even if these links can take on a diversity of forms. There is however one more or less direct link between religion and agrarian ecosystems. In countries with temperate or tropical forests, polytheism is resonant with the sounds of an environment where everything can appear menacing. Desert areas, on the other hand, are dominated by silence. As Ernest Renan wrote, not in a racist way but admiringly, as demonstrated by Perrine Simon-Nahum, "the desert is monotheistic[21]".

The desert ecosystem, while not deterministic, seems to be more conducive to monotheism. This link between nature and deities is already found in Greek mythology. For example, Dionysus is the god of wine and grapevines, Artemis (Diana for the Romans) is the goddess of hunting, and Demeter is the goddess of agriculture. The deities are the expression of this osmosis between man and nature.

The main characteristic of agrarian societies is that they are subject to climate uncertainty. How often it rains or whether the rivers will flood is the core uncertainty and it is water-related. Without water, there will be neither crops nor pasture. But this uncertainty differs from one agrarian system to another. To manage these uncertainties, agrarian societies may adopt multiple deities, build communal granaries, diversify their crops or instate authoritarian water management systems. Thus there is a link between the agrarian ecosystem, the political system and the religious system, even if this earth–politics–heavens relationship is not automatic.

Nomadic and livestock systems whose survival depends on the arrival of the wet season have high levels of uncertainty. The rains determine how much pasture will be available to feed the animals. The most frequently adopted strategy to manage climate uncertainty is to diversify herds and move them around. Be it fact or legend, the story of Abraham, circa 1800 BC, symbolises this mobility: "Yahweh said to Abram, 'Go forth from your native land.' [...] Abram went forth as Yahweh had commanded him, and Lot went with him. Abram was seventy-five years old when he left Haran" (in north-western Mesopotamia) to set out for the land of Canaan (Gen. 12:1–4). For nomadic herders, mobility is the ultimate source of food security[22]. The population of Palestine between the eleventh and sixth century BC was predominantly comprised of nomadic and sedentary clans[23].

Grain-based societies, be it wheat as in the Middle East or rice as in China, are exposed to another system of uncertainty. Very often, there is only one harvest per year, with uncertain yields. This uncertainty has regularly led to the establishment of centralized States as a means of protecting against scarcity. In certain cases, political centralization led to monotheism, as at the time of King David in the eleventh century BC.

Periods of drought triggered population movements across the entire Fertile Crescent, as in the story of Joseph, whose brothers sold him only to encounter him again when a famine forced them to travel to Egypt (Gen. 41:53–42:7). In around 1500 BC, the state of Egypt was centrally managing food uncertainty by using public granaries. In Genesis, it is written that Joseph, the son of Jacob, descended from Abraham, became the overseer of the Egyptian Pharaoh's royal granaries. He "stored the grain" to avoid famine in Egypt (Gen. 41:33–49), and saved his family from hunger. The Old Testament is full of accounts of omnipresent food uncertainty and the importance of grain, as in the book of Ruth, which is about famine, harvesting, gleaning and barley. State-level grain storage protects against famine.

This same link between uncertainty and centralizing States is present in hydraulic societies where everyone both upstream and downstream must be guaranteed access to water when it is scarce, as in China, Mesopotamia, Madagascar (as we saw with Andrianampoinimerina at the start of this book) or in pre-Colombian Mexico[24]. The function of grain-states, or of the Philistine and Greco-Roman "city-states" that depended on their agricultural hinterland, is equally to collect taxes from farmers and to guarantee water access for all, protect their subjects from famine and from invasion by "nomadic barbarians"[25].

Many centuries later, the system of grain uncertainty had not changed. In the third-century-AD Roman Empire, "The rich alone could also defeat time [...] Those who could store the surplus of the harvest by gathering it into their granaries were the ones who could take advantage, every year, of this rise in prices [...] Not surprisingly, therefore, granaries emerge as the economic villains of the ancient world [...] wealth was widely thought of as lying in the hands of the gods[26]". This text confirms the importance of polytheism as a system of social security.

Conversely, agrarian systems that rely on tubers such as cassava, which grows in forests or in savanna woodlands, are far less conducive to the emergence of a centralized political system and monotheism. Once cassava reaches maturity, it can be harvested year round for one or two years, as was done in Congo from the sixteenth century AD. The soil serves as a natural granary[27]. Root and tuber societies enjoy regular harvests year round and do not need to store food reserves in collective granaries. Hence, they have less-centralized political systems that leave more room for local deities, village systems or city-states.

Now that we have taken this detour through the intrinsic uncertainties in nomadic and sedentary agrarian systems, we can better understand why part of the Hebrew population were not in favour of replacing polytheism with monotheism. Switching to monotheism left them with more of the uncertainty to carry when it came to their food security. In order to make such a change acceptable, their new god would have to be far more powerful than the old deities, something the prophets work to demonstrate all throughout the Old Testament.

The Strategic Dimension of the Choice Between Polytheism and Monotheism

In the Book of Jeremiah, likely written during or shortly before the Babylonian Captivity in the sixth century BC, we find the Jews who remained in Judea complaining that they are no longer allowed to worship other gods: "But ever since we stopped making offerings to the Queen of Heaven [a popular Jewish deity] and pouring libations to her, we have lacked everything, and we have been consumed by the sword and by famine" (Jer. 44:18). For the Jews, there is a link of cause and effect between their suffering and the fact that they no longer make sacrifices to the Queen of Heaven, a deity in polytheism.

This conception is very close to the Greek conception prior to the Hellenistic period, which began in the fourth century BC. The farmer is instructed "when he sets his hand to the plough, to pray to Zeus in the earth and to holy Demeter, that the ears of Demeter's corn may be heavy and ripe[28]". This is similar to the Christian rogation rituals of praying for a good harvest. To be meaningful, a religion must be effective and useful.

This tension is relatively easy to explain from a strategic-anthropology perspective. Choosing polytheism and opting to worship multiple gods is a strategic choice, although probably more implicit than conscious. Having a diversity of protective deities is a way for the imagination to minimize the very real risks of disease or famine. As the prophet Isaiah himself points out, "Who would fashion a god or cast a statue that can do no good?" (Isa. 44:10). He makes the link between a deity and its expected effect, between its usefulness and its meaning.

Polytheism is like an *à la carte* life insurance, a way to avoid putting all one's gods in the same basket when it comes to climate risks such as droughts or floods, which mean famine. If one god is not effective, another can be chosen until one is found that solves our day-to-day problems. Surrendering polytheism is very risky as it could lead to the loss of a divine protection.

In his novel *The Long Ships*, Swedish author Frans G. Bengtsson portrays the meeting of polytheism, Islam and Christianity 1500 years later in the tenth century AD. The Vikings are facing the same problems as the fifth-century-BC Jews, wondering to which saint they should devote themselves. The hero Orm has been captured by the Arabs and is held captive in the south of Muslim Spain. He wonders which god is the most powerful in this land. In Scandinavia, the strongest is Thor and the wisest is Odin. However, as he admits, "Perchance it may be that our gods wield but little power in this land [Muslim Andalusia]; therefore, lord, I for my part shall willingly obey your command and worship your god." He becomes a Muslim in a Muslim land. Later, on returning home, Orm discovers that the Kingdom of Denmark has become Christian. He observes that certain Vikings do not see this as progress, and have claimed that "the harvest was smaller and the cows' milk thinner nowadays, and that this was because people had begun to neglect the old gods[29]". Changing religious systems is not without its risks.

This is why believers in either a polytheist or monotheist religion need miracles, signs and wonders that denote how effective the god or gods can be on a practical level. Even in Judaism, God, Yahweh, speaking through the prophet Isaiah, points out that "It is I [...] who annul the omens of diviners, and make fools of the augurs; who turn sages back and make nonsense of their knowledge but confirm the word of My servant and fulfill the prediction of My messengers" (Isa. 44:25–26). Thus the god of Israel, of the Kenites, is presented as being the most effective. The Christian New Testament recounts Jesus' many miracles, starting with the transformation of water into wine at the wedding at Cana at the outset of his public life (John 2:1–12). As Étienne Nodet and Justin Taylor have written: "Jesus was a teacher and a healer. Later on, Peter, Barnabas and even Paul can all be seen performing healing and excorcisms[30]". Thus, the success of a new religion depends in part on evidence of its effectiveness and the political power of its proponent. As Jean Soler says when discussing human inventions, and particularly monotheism, "it is about utility, not truth". They are meant to help us "better adapt to the surrounding environment[31]".

This reminds us that religion is a magico-religious system. It is an invariant. What varies from one era to another is the proportion of magic, which is more of the people, to religious, linked more to the elite. This system combines a belief with practices that solve day-to-day problems in an agrarian ecosystem. Within that space, farmers such as Cane and herders such as Abel coexist in varying degrees of conflict (see Gen. 4:1–16), and all of this is linked to a more or less centralized political power.

Only an Almighty God Can Make Monotheism Acceptable

Monotheism demands belief in a single god, but that god must be all powerful, recognized as being superior to all other deities, to make up for the loss of divine diversity. In some ways, this one god must have a monopoly on divine legitimacy. This power can be linked to the power of a State or of cities, as in Zoroastrianism which was linked to the Babylonian kingdoms between the tenth and fourth century BC. This link between monotheism and State is not an automatic one: the Roman Empire was centralized, at least from the time of Augustus (63 BC to 14 AD) and polytheistic. Subsequent Roman emperors became more inclined towards a form of monotheism around a sun god, which served their efforts to further centralize their political power.

This is why, as a strategy, monotheism is more risky, because it leaves far less leeway to select the best possible protection against day to day hardship. A single God can be more powerful and hence potentially more protective, but there is no certainty that this God will be absolutely effective. Can one God take care of everything: births, harvests, diseases, career success? Can God protect the righteous against misfortune? That is the question in the biblical book of Job, written after the return from the Babylonian Captivity. If the political power on which the single God relies collapses, then the God's power collapses with it. Polytheism is more flexible, thanks to its range of deities. It offers "better" protection against geopolitical and climate risks.

Even if the sixteenth-century maxim of *cuius regio, eius religio* ("whose realm, their religion"), which affirms that the religion of a territory and its inhabitants shall be that of its ruling power, had not been invented yet, in practice there was indeed a link between monotheism or polytheism and political power. When the Judeans conquered Idumea south of Jerusalem in the second century BC, they forcibly converted and circumcised the Idumeans. This practice appeared "normal" in the political context of the time. In the fifth century AD, when Clovis, "king of the Franks[32]", was baptized, several thousand of his warriors followed suit.

This choice between multiple religious options is all the more strategic given that polytheism will easily incorporate a monotheistic god into its pantheon of deities because this adds an additional asset to its "social security" system, whereas monotheism does not accept other deities. This difference caused tensions between the Jews and the Greek then Roman authorities who did not understand this "sectarianism" towards their polytheistic security system. "For the Romans, the Jews as Judeo-Christians were monotheistic foreigners from the East who rejected the Empire's cult[33]." Abandoning polytheism represented a significant risk to the survival of the group, the city and the Empire.

This partly explains why polytheistic political regimes harassed the monotheistic Jews and Christians whenever they refused to include elements of the Greek or Roman pantheon into their religion. They felt that their survival or their legitimacy was threatened. It was not until Constantine's reign in the fourth century AD that Christianity became widespread throughout the Roman Empire. Another monotheistic religion emerged contemporaneously in Persia (modern Iran), where the Sasanian King Shapur II recognized "Mazdaism [monotheism/henotheism] as the State religion[34]". In the fourth century AD, monotheism appears to have been in fashion.

A link is also probable between belief in a single, almighty God and the believers' agenda of "converting" other nations. This is what the prophet Isaiah says in the Bible, in the section known as "second Isaiah" (or Deutero-Isaiah), as he quotes Yahweh's words: "They have no knowledge, who carry the wood of their carved image, and pray to a god that cannot save. Tell and bring forth your case; [...] Look to Me, and be saved, all you ends of the earth! For I am God, and there is no other" (Isa. 45:20–22).

This strategy of expanding to the "ends of the earth" was not a given. Part of the Jews were against any form of proselytism. The very existence of Jewish proselytism is disputed. However, again from a strategic standpoint, assuming that protecting territory and ensuring a people's survival are the priorities behind actors' strategies, proselytizing seems quite rational.

An almighty god must correspond to a larger and wealthier territory, which in turn means that populations are better protected. This was King David's strategy when he conquered the land of Canaan to form the Kingdom of Israel with a single God, Yahweh, a thousand years before the common era. It was also the Jews' strategy from the fourth century BC onwards. The more believers we have, the more powerful we are.

*

The Jewish people were divided into several groups, some of which were in favour of spreading Judaism and others against. The prophet Isaiah recalled, slightly before or after the destruction of the First Temple of Jerusalem in 586 BC by the Babylonian king Nebuchadnezzar II, that Yahweh, God, had said to Israel: "I will also make you a light of nations, that My salvation may reach the ends of the earth" (Isa. 49:6). This passage confirms that Judaism was already universalistic, if not proselytizing, well before the first century AD[35].

When it comes to the spread of innovations, proselytism is one of the invariant mechanisms that anthropology brings to light by looking beyond the particularities of the innovation in question. Advertising can be understood as the modern form of this invariant mechanism, which is focussed on persuasion.

Proselytism is itself the product of mobility, another constant of innovation processes. Mobility is linked to war, trade and the exile of the Jewish elite. It allows cultures to mix, which is itself a source of transformation and innovation, which can be positive or negative depending on the position of different groups in society. This is often what the term globalization is referring to today.

Most of the time it is very difficult to find a single origin for an innovation because it is the outcome of a process of cross-fertilization. It is also the result of numerous tensions, power relations and various political and military impositions. In order to spread, it must also show signs of its effectiveness, in the form of miracles. If the miracles are not convincing, then coercion is used, particularly military force.

Like any invention, monotheism is the result of both continuity and a series of discontinuities, of structural effects and those of actors, of transgressions and reinterpretations of the original invention. Its spread is not linear. Hunter-gatherers became sedentary and then became hunter-gatherers again, as James C. Scott shows[36]. Mesopotamia went through phases of monotheism and polytheism.

This transformation and gradual spread of monotheism can be observed from the polytheistic Hellenization of Judea in the fourth century onwards. Then, from the late-first and second century AD, this innovation was driven by the Christian Jews, who invoked a rabbi named Jesus who was in favour of proselytism. While its future was not guaranteed, there were many conditions in place for monotheism to progress further.

~ ~ ~

Chapter 3

The Hellenization and Romanization of the Mediterranean Rim

In the fourth century BC, a geopolitical event transformed most of the polytheistic societies around the Mediterranean rim. Alexander the Great (356–323 BC) conquered northern Greece as far as the Danube, Egypt and the Nile in the southern Mediterranean, and then Syria and Mesopotamia to the east, between the Tigris and Euphrates, and as far as the Indus in present-day Pakistan.

The three hundred years preceding the emergence of Christianity were a period of both greatness and political instability for Palestine. The construction of the Second Temple began with the return from the Babylonian Captivity in the sixth century BC. King Herod began an extension of the Temple at the end of the first century BC, in the Greco-Roman style. Construction would last until the seventh decade of the first century AD. The Temple's architecture was one of the most visible signs of the Hellenization of Jewish culture and thus of its integration into a more global world than that of Judea, Galilee and Samaria. Monotheistic Judea was a tiny dot in the polytheistic Roman Empire, but it was in full demographic boom and a transit point between the northern and southern Mediterranean.

The Hellenistic Matrix of the Jewish Diaspora

Military conquests, trade expansion and belief spreading can all be understood as forms of proselytism, which functions based on three main bioenergies[1]: hydraulic energy from seas and rivers, human energy—which explains why slavery lasted so long, from the emergence of States and agriculture until coal energy brought the industrial revolution in the eighteenth century[2]—and animal energy, in particular from donkeys, horses and camels[3].

As a reminder of the importance of bioenergy, I have chosen a passage from Genesis that exemplifies nomadic life. It is written that the Pharaoh gave Abraham, the ancestor of the Jewish, Christian and Muslim religions, "sheep, oxen, male donkeys, male and female servants, female donkeys, and camels" (Gen. 12:16). Bioenergy is what fuelled the spread of nomadic mobility and underpinned the logistics of Hellenization, thanks to military control of land and river routes. In turn, Hellenization would provide the framework for the spread of Jewish culture and later of Roman and Christian cultures.

This matrix was also linguistic in nature, thanks to *koinè* (the common language, κοινὴ διάλεκτος), the Greek lingua franca of the time– the equivalent of today's *"globish*[4]*" (global English)*. Linguistic exchanges were so extensive that the Torah was translated into Greek in the third century BC, under Ptolemy. It became known as the Septuagint because it was said to have been translated by seventy-two scholars, probably in Alexandria, which had a large Jewish community. It helped unite the Jewish diaspora and was an important tool for their proselytism. Later on, as Christianity was developing, the Greek philosophical influence was also present, with Plotinus (205–270), a Greco-Roman neoplatonic philosopher based in Rome, as we will see in Chapter 8.

The predominant use of the Greek language over Aramaic, which was spoken in Judea, Galilee and Samaria, empowered and supported the spread of what would later become Hellenistic Jewish Christianity and then Christianity. It is quite likely that without the original Judeans and converts who formed the Jewish diaspora, many of whom spoke and read Greek, the Christian invention would not have become an innovation. The prevalence of the Greek *koinè* confirms the strong link between an innovation's ability to spread beyond its culture of origin and the existence of a language of international communication, what is known today as soft power, a "soft way" of extending influence.

The Spread of Jewish Monotheism During the Roman Climatic Optimum

At the end of the fourth century BC, after the death of Alexander the Great, his generals reorganized the Macedonian Empire into different kingdoms, including one in Egypt that would be ruled by the Ptolemaic dynasty from its capital in Alexandria, and another in Syria by the Seleucid dynasty, with Antioch as its capital. They each in turn ruled over the Kingdom of Judea before the arrival of the Romans. Following a period of independence between 164 and 63 BC, Jerusalem and Judea were retaken by Pompey in 63 BC and the kingdom then became a Roman protectorate.

Control of Judea was strategic for the Greek then Roman authorities. It was the route that connected Mesopotamia to North Africa and more specifically to Egypt, which thanks to the Nile floods was one of the breadbaskets of Rome and the Mediterranean. Wheat was one of the major geopolitical issues of the time. The survival of societies depended on it. In Rome, the phrase *"Panem et circenses"* ("Bread and circuses") was not taken lightly. No wheat, no bread. No bread, no peace in society.

The Romans reclaimed the Mediterranean from Greek domination and called it *Mare nostrum*, "our sea". It became the logistical foundation of Rome's power and the space in which commercial, military, intellectual and cultural exchanges developed. It allowed the religious invention of Jewish monotheism to deploy across a polytheistic world that would eventually tip into Christian monotheism in the fourth century AD. Thus, the social process that spread the monotheistic innovation lasted six to eight centuries, as fast as the bioenergies would allow.

The Roman Empire's prosperity corresponded to a climatic period known as the Roman Climatic Optimum (RCO), also known as the Roman Warm Period. The RCO was partly behind Roman power and wealth from the second century BC[5] until the second century AD, when the empire began to enter a crisis phase[6]. On the opposite side of Eurasia, in China, the Han dynasty (206 BC to 220 AD) underwent a similar period of geographical and political expansion[7]. The period of global warming brought abundant wheat in the West and rice in the East. According to Professor Alain Préat, a doctor of geology, temperatures during the RCO rose by around 2°C[8]. The data are disputed but very interesting nonetheless because they broaden the field of analysis of innovation processes.

Echoes of the RCO climate debate still resonate today, and regardless of how it is ultimately settled, the important thing to remember is that climate, solar cycles, volcanoes, floods and pandemics are part of the tide of history in general and of the history of innovations in particular[9]. They have long been an invisible form of globalization. As in Roman times, today's global warming affects the East as much as the West. Similarly, the current COVID-19 pandemic spread from China through Europe to the United States. The processes of innovation and societal change are embedded in geopolitics and the transformation of environmental and health systems.

The process that spread monotheism continued thanks to the Hellenization and then the Romanization of a wide coastal area of the Mediterranean, as well as along the Red Sea[10], one of the maritime routes towards India and China. It also continued to spread via the great rivers, the Nile, the Jordan, the Tigris and the Euphrates. They served as vectors transferring people, goods and ideas between East and West, bolstered by the military strength of the Roman legions.

The Reconstruction of the Temple Under Herod and the Hellenization of the Jewish Elite

The city of Jerusalem and its temple were seen as the centre of the world by a religion that had universal ambitions, as we have already seen with the second Isaiah. At the start of the Common Era, Jerusalem was a fairly large city for its time, even if there were several much larger ones. It would have had about 80,000 inhabitants and an agricultural hinterland. By comparison, Alexandria—the largest city in the Greek world and founded by Alexander the Great in 331 BC—had around 500,000 inhabitants and Antioch had 300,000, and both had large Jewish populations. First-century-AD Rome is estimated to have had 50,000 Jews.

Being a place of pilgrimage, Jerusalem was a wealthy city because the pilgrims, some of whom were of the Diaspora, paid tithes to the Temple priests. The Romans seized the Temple's riches on several occasions before it was finally destroyed. Jerusalem also collected taxes for Rome. Like all territories in the Empire[11], it provided revenue for the Romans[12]. The various empires of the East and then the West constantly sought control over this key corridor—which connected the north of the Fertile Crescent, Mesopotamia, to the south—and its capital, Jerusalem, overlooking the River Jordan[13].

As a result of these successive political dominations, part of the Judean elite developed forms of acculturation to Greek culture, which in turn led opponents of this elite to attempt to purify Judean culture on numerous occasions. These efforts were combined with various Judean-led political liberation struggles, such as the Maccabean Revolt (which later brought about the Hasmonean dynasty) in the second century BC. Then, in the first century AD, there was the Zealot movement, centered more around Galilee. These political struggles included a religious dimension, namely the fight against polytheism.

In 37 BC, following numerous battles and a series of victories and setbacks, and with the support of Octavian, who would become Caesar Augustus in 27 BC[14], Herod the Great became King of the Jews (37–4 BC.). He was not from Judea but from Idumaea, southwest of the Dead Sea, a region that had been conquered and forcibly converted by the high priest John Hyrcanus, a descendant of the Maccabees and part of the Hasmonean dynasty[15]. John Hyrcanus ruled Judea from 134 to 104 BC. Étienne Nodet and Justin Taylor add that his son Aristobulus "did the same with the Ituraeans" to the north (in what is now Lebanon), and his successor Alexander Jannaeus followed suit in the cities he conquered[16]. These events remind us that innovations are not always adopted voluntary. Staying with the anthropological viewpoint, apart from "early adopters"[17] who voluntarily embrace them, it is likely that most innovations are imposed de facto on the rest of the population affected by the change, either by force or by imitation[18] and therefore by mimicry. Faith in a religion has a strong collective dimension.

In the first century BC, Herod the Great expanded and embellished the temple in Jerusalem but established his capital further north, in Caesarea, on the coast, with a hippodrome and an amphitheatre, on the model of Greco-Roman cities. He was one of the representatives of this new Jewish cosmopolitan culture open to "modernity" that was in conflict with "traditional" Jews.

During Herod's reign, tensions continued between, on the one hand, the priestly caste, many of whom were Sadducees who admired Greek architecture and lavish decors and supported "the concentration of sacerdotal and military power assumed by the Hasmoneans [King Herod][19]", and on the other hand, the more austere Pharisees, who sought to uphold the purity of Jewish Law.

The high priest who ran the Temple was appointed by King Herod and was the head of the priestly caste. He was the highest traditional authority[20] and had to be a descendant of Aaron—a member of the Tribe of Levi. He presided over the *Sanhedrin* (*bet din* in Hebrew), which among other things had policing powers, but not the power to impose the death penalty, which only the Romans could do, as the historian Reza Aslan points out[21]. The Temple of Jerusalem was clearly a high place of symbolic, political and religious significance dominated by the priests.

The Maccabean Revolt and the Question of Eternal Life (Second Century BC)

There was both resonance and tension between Greek and Judean culture. In 165 BC, Antiochus IV—the Seleucid king of Syria, Mesopotamia and Anatolia, north of Judea, and vanquisher of the Lagid Dynasty of Egypt—sought to impose an altar in the Second Temple of Jerusalem to be dedicated to Zeus (Ζεύς), a Greek god who the Romans would later deem akin to their god Jupiter. For the monotheistic Jews, contrary to the polytheistic Greek and Romans, this was a desecration. Combined with a contested tax policy, it sparked revolt among the Maccabees (175–140 BC), who recaptured Jerusalem. The city remained independent until 63 BC.

The Maccabean Revolt is well known historically. What is perhaps less well known is the theological question it raised and that would remain at the heart of Judeo-Christian debates: how can we explain that people who follow the law of God, in this case the Maccabees—who were respecting the Shabbat day when the Seleucids of Syria attacked and massacred them—should die because of the very fact that they were following this law (1 Macc. 2:29–38)?

The First Book of Maccabees (1 Macc.) is thought to have been written around 100 BC, first in Hebrew and then in its Greek translation. The Second Book of Maccabees (2 Macc.) dates from around 124 BC. Only Catholics consider these two books as canonical, while Protestant and Jewish traditions do not. Orthodox Christians, on the other hand, recognize all four Books of Maccabees. The story later retained by the Catholic tradition in the Second Book of Maccabees is that of a family of seven brothers and their mother were arrested and tortured by King Antiochus IV Epiphanes, the Seleucid King of Syria, for refusing to "eat pork" (2 Macc. 7:1). The story of the Maccabees is, in a way, a response to the Book of Job (fifth century BC), in which it is written: "But man, if he dies, remains inert; when a human being dies, where is he? But mortals languish and die; Man expires; where is he? [...] If a man dies, can he live again?" (Job 14:10 and 14). In the Jewish tradition of the time, before the first century BC, death meant going to Sheol, from which one does not return. There was no resurrection and no eternal life. The psalmist asks God not to "abandon [him] to Sheol" (Ps. 16:10). There is therefore a contradiction between respecting divine law and dying because of it and thus ending up in Sheol, a kingdom of darkness, especially if one is young.

The Second Book of Maccabees refers to the "resurrection of bodies", as the French translators of the Bible de Jérusalem (1956) write in a note on page 580: "With his last breath he said: 'You accursed fiend [Antiochus IV], you are depriving us of this present life, but the King of the universe will raise us up to live again forever, because we are dying for his laws'." (2 Macc. 7:9).

The matter of resurrection of the dead was a debate that would last for several centuries, and particularly during the period when Jesus was preaching. He believed in resurrection, as did the Pharisees, a movement within Judaism to which he was close. Conversely, the Sadducees rejected resurrection. In the part of the Book of Daniel written in the second century BC, we can already read: "Many of those that sleep in the dust of the earth will awake, some to eternal life, others to reproaches, to everlasting abhorrence" (Dan. 12:2).

Resurrection and eternal life are a useful way of attempting to resolve the issue of righteous people who suffer or die when following God's law. It gives meaning to daily suffering with a promise of reward in the afterlife. With Paul the Apostle (Saint Paul), resurrection took on a messianic and apocalyptic meaning of release from earthly suffering through the return of Jesus, the risen Messiah. Resurrection offers a solution to earthly suffering by imagining a heavenly afterlife.

This shows that for an innovation to be successfully received despite the obstacles, it must solve some of the problems of everyday life, which resurrection (life after death) does, at least in the religious imagination. By re-enchanting the afterlife, resurrection as presented by the Pharisees and by Paul gives meaning to life on earth, especially if that life is difficult and overly uncertain.

*

At the start of the first century AD, there was still no rabbinate. The figure of the rabbi emerged between the first and second centuries AD and eventually gave rise to rabbinic Judaism. The important point to remember is that in the first century AD, Judaism was expanding. It was well represented and organized in Asia Minor as well as in the western Mediterranean, where Jewish communities existed as far away as Lyon. There was much theological debate among these communities, who had no easy access to the Temple and gathered around the synagogues, whose role was strengthened by the destruction of the Temple. They had the same function as a forum for debate among Pharisaic Rabbinic or Judeo-Christian Jewish communities (Jews who followed James the Just, the brother of Jesus, while respecting circumcision, kashrut, Shabbat, etc.[22]), Hellenistic Christian Jews (Jews of Greek culture) and Pagan-Christians (pagans who followed Jesus without following the Torah, and who were known as "God-fearers").

None of these terms are stabilized. They are primarily descriptive and indicate a general trend: the transition from Jewish culture to Christian Jewish culture, then its transformation into a Hellenistic Christian Jewish culture and then to a Greco-Roman Christian culture, all in a nonlinear and often chaotic way. For now, we are still at the end of the first century BC. Jesus has not yet been born. The Temple priests are a "high-street name", to use an illustrative anachronism. There is much debate among Jews about circumcision and proselytism.

~ ~ ~

Chapter 4

Two Great Debates in the Jewish World: Circumcision and Proselytism

Hellenization created significant tension within Jewish society that extended well beyond Palestine, because it drove the transformation of urban lifestyles along the lines of Greek and then Greco-Roman cities. As it led to the mixing of populations in public life, it disrupted the traditional Jewish rules of purity that held that an uncircumcised person was impure. Because the Greeks were not circumcised, how could one mix with them and adopt their practices if circumcision is compulsory? Circumcision and proselytizing were all the more contentious because both issues touched upon the Greek polytheistic and Jewish monotheistic identities.

Circumcision and the Greek Gymnasia: An Identity Issue

When they introduced gymnasia around the second century BC, Greek royalty imported a new practice specific to its culture, namely complete nudity in the stadiums. This created a problem for the circumcised Jews, because "the Greeks, who accepted public nudity, radically rejected circumcision, because what they considered repugnant was not the fact of showing the penis, but of uncovering the glans[1]". As historian Simon Schama writes: "The circumcised penis prompted cackles of derision from the Greeks whose pride in the lengthy, tapered prepuce can be seen on innumerable vases and amphorae[2]." The Romans were as repulsed as the Greeks. Above all, Simon Claude Mimouni notes that circumcised Jews were banned from Roman gymnasia and baths, which is why some members of the Jewish elite tried to hide their circumcision through a practice that Paul the Apostle would later call "epispasm[3]".

There is a historical trace[4] of it from the second century BC in the First Book of Maccabbees, where we read that the Seleucid King Antiochus IV "authorized them to introduce the ordinances of the Gentiles. Thereupon they built a gymnasium in Jerusalem according to the Gentile custom. They disguised their circumcision and abandoned the holy covenant; they allied themselves with the Gentiles and sold themselves to wrongdoing" (1 Macc. 1:13–15).

Circumcision was not unique to the Jewish world. It was practised in many countries around the eastern Mediterranean. However, according to Simon Claude Mimouni, it seems to have been unknown among Indo-European peoples. The issue of circumcision was very divisive within Judaism itself, particularly between the urban elite, more favourable to Greek practices, and the rural population.

Between the second century BC of the Maccabees and the first century AD of Paul the Apostle, choosing for or against circumcision proved to be a strategic element in the spread of the Jewish monotheistic innovation and then the Jewish-Christian one. Retaining circumcision was a major constraint that could impede the widespread diffusion of Jewish Christianity across the Greek and Roman world, while at the same time many Jews considered it a core element of their cultural and religious identity[5]. It touches on the fundamental question of purity. For part of the Jewish people of the time, being uncircumcised meant being unclean. Eating with the uncircumcised meant becoming unclean, and becoming unclean meant being excluded from the community. To be unclean led to social death.

At the same time, paradoxically, during the "golden age" of Palestine[6] between the second century BC and the third century AD, part of the pagan population was drawn to the Jewish religion:

> The Sabbath rest, the concept of reward and punishment, the belief in an afterlife, and above all the transcendent hope of resurrection were enticing features that persuaded many people to adopt the Jewish faith[7].

Hence some Jews faced the following dilemma: either abandon circumcision so as to integrate Greek modernity but in so doing become impure and risk being excluded from their own community, as happened to the Christian Jews who opposed circumcision in the first century AD; or preserve their collective Jewish identity at the cost of some degree of separation from the modern Greek and Roman world.

A portion of Jews, probably of the Diaspora, was in favour of Judaism spreading in the cities around the Mediterranean and in the Middle East. This is why in the first century AD, Paul the Apostle, who represented the Diaspora's Hellenized Jews who followed Jesus and the Torah, advocated abandoning imposing this ritual constraint on the pagans. It was hindering the monotheistic innovation's progress. An innovation will have difficulty spreading if the actors receiving it feel that the novelty threatens their professional, cultural or gender identity. This was the case with circumcision, which threatened Greek identity, and non-circumcision, which threatened Jewish identity.

Jewish Proselytism and the Expansion of Jewish Communities With or Without Missionaries

The existence of Jewish proselytism is disputed[8], a debate that has a bearing on contemporary questions about the origins of the Jewish people, because proselytism means accepting that people who are not of Jewish descent can become Jewish by converting. This is a sensitive topic because it points to the absence of a single "pure" origin of the Jewish people.

And yet there are a number of arguments that support the existence of proselytism and the resulting interbreeding of Jewish populations with other groups. The first form of proselytism was historical and authoritarian . The second was demographic. The third flowed from the attraction that the "God-fearing" pagans had for the Jewish religion. The fourth relates to the practical matter of marriage between a Jew and a non-Jew, especially in the Diaspora.

The first historical form is linked to the Jewish military conquests of the second century BC. This proselytism was authoritarian and it escalated under the Maccabees' Hasmonean dynasty, as we have already seen with John Hyrcan and the forced conversion of the region south of Judea. For the historian Simon Schama, the Maccabees did rise up "against the cultural and physical annihilations of the crazed Antiochus IV, but it took barely more than a generation for them to morph from rebels to players in the Seleucid world" and become "great forced converters, idol-smashers and tearers-down of pagan altars (as well as the temple of the [Jewish] Samaritans on Mount Gerizim)"[9].

The second argument that supports the existence of proselytism is demographic. Various historians estimate that between 50 and 150 AD, the population of the Roman Empire was between 70 and 75 million[10]. The Empire's Jewish population, according to various sources, is estimated at 4 to 6 million, and at 2 million further east in the Empire[11]. In that same era, Judea had between 500,000 and 1 million inhabitants[12]. It seems, therefore, that the increase in the Jewish population cannot be explained solely by a rapidly rising birth rate. Non-Jews were being integrated into the Jewish population. As in most societies, the dominant "ethnic group" has no one pure origin. Between 6 % and 8 % of the population of the Roman Empire were Jewish, so they constituted a large group.

For Étienne Nodet and Justin Taylor, "this healthy demography was due to two factors: natural growth and the arrival of proselytes", particularly in Egypt and Syria[13]. According to Étienne Nodet, this proselytism would not have relied on sending missionaries to the pagans, but rather on attracting sympathizers to the Jewish religion. Nodet and Taylor believe that there was also internal proselytism within Judaism itself, such as by John the Baptist, who baptized Jesus in the Jordan, or by the Zealots and the Pharisees. The two authors also point to forms of proselytism in the Diaspora synagogues and in some public squares (agora, ἀγορά), mainly in Alexandria and Antioch, cities with large Jewish communities: They "welcomed many proselytes and well-wishers, who were integrated into the people, but there is no suggestion that this was the result of an organized mission among the Gentiles[14]."

The historian Enrico Norelli also wonders if "there was a missionary Judaism, and if so, how intense was it?". He believes there was, referring to Jesus' diatribe against the Pharisees who "travel land and sea to win one proselyte" (Matt. 23:15). The 1956 *Bible de Jérusalem* adds in a note that "Jewish propaganda in the Greco-Roman world was very active" (p. 1320). However, according to Enrico Norelli, this missionary movement was "nothing like the missionary drive of those who believed in Jesus[15]". This dynamic indicates a strategic choice by a fraction of the Jewish people, as we shall see later.

Didier Long appears to confirm the existence of a form of "expansionist" Judaism when he shows that there were *apostoli*, that is to say, "plenipotentiary envoys from a parent community, Jerusalem or Babylon, overseeing the dogmatic unity and financial circuits of local communities under their jurisdiction". For Didier Long, the *apostoli*, or apostles, who took up the teachings of Jesus, reprised an itinerant missionary model that already existed in the Jewish world[16].

No matter how intense the missionary movement was, it is plausible that *social networks* existed in the form of *apostoli* or, at a more sociological level, in the form of family and trade networks. They would constitute the logistical and social matrix for the spread of the Jewish and then Christian monotheistic innovation[17]. These networks were the consequence of the various displacements and deportations of part of the Jewish population. According to the historian Mario Liverani, "The totals of more than 40,000 deportees from Israel [the northern kingdom], and about 200,000 from Judah [southern kingdom], given in the Assyrian annals, seem to be realistic (for more populated areas the numbers are much greater) and constitute a significant percentage of the population. [The vacuum left behind was] compensated by deportation from other provinces to the newly conquered one[18]". The other Jewish communities developed from the migration of traders and artisans to the major Mediterranean cities.

There were many Jewish communities in all the territories controlled by the Greek Lagid and Seleucid dynasties, in Cyrenaica, Asia Minor and beyond, in Antioch, Damascus, Ephesus, Athens, Thessalonica[19], Corinth and Rome[20]. A large share of the letters written by Paul the Apostle in the first century AD were addressed to Jewish, Hellenistic Christian Jewish and Pagan-Christian communities in these cities. These cities were also home to the synagogues that, after the destruction of the Temple, were where rabbinic Judaism developed, along with its different religious tendencies, including the one that embraced Jesus.

The fourth reason that can explain Jewish proselytism is marriage. Etienne Nodet and Justin Taylor write that "Marriage with a non-Jew also required the other's conversion for validity[21]". This was therefore also a form of coercive proselytism that may have mostly affected gentile women marrying Jews.

Hence, it would seem highly probable that Jewish proselytism existed, while its nature and practices remain disputed[22]. It is possible that these conversions were not as voluntary as they were for the future Christian Jews of Greek culture, who would drive the expansion of monotheism in a world that, we must remember, was polytheistic and opposed to the monotheistic invention because it did not integrate Greco-Roman deities.

In order to spread, an innovation needs a network of actors to carry it. An idea does not spread just by virtue of being good, or "logical", or rational, or "coherent", but also because social groups spend a lot of energy making sure it is successful. There is no mechanical link between the content of an innovation and its spread. A "bad" innovation can spread just as well as a "good" innovation. However, the more developed the network, the greater the capacity to carry the innovation. A society is not made up of atomized individuals, but of collective networks.

The different factions of the Jewish people were divided on the issue of proselytism. Those who advocated it disagreed over whether to require circumcision, compliance with the dietary rules of kashrut, and purification through ritual baths in order to be recognized as Jewish. As we have already seen, this means that not everyone in the Jewish diaspora was circumcised or followed kashrut. These debates continued throughout the invention of Christianity between the first and fourth century AD.

All figures on Jewish demographics around the first century AD should be treated with caution, but they indicate that the increase in the number of Jews in the eastern and western Mediterranean cannot be explained solely by natural population growth and the various exiles. This means that monotheistic Judaism was an expanding, proselytizing religion open to a form of conversion, and perhaps also missionary, just as monotheistic Christianity and then Islam would be.

The *Pax Romana* and the Rise of Messianic Movements in Israel

Not all the historical elements outlined above are a matter of consensus. However, they were all in place at the time of the invention of Christianity: geopolitical changes, the networks[23] of the Jewish diaspora, the social classes, the synagogues, varying degrees of proselytism and the ambivalent combination of an apocalyptic imaginary and Messianism. These elements would encourage the mobility of people, goods and beliefs, thanks to cultural Hellenization, the creation of a common language, Koine Greek, and the translation of the Torah into Greek.

As is often the case in history, geopolitics was a factor of change, whether through Hellenization, wars, international trade, such as the silk roads, or "royal marriages[24]". More-recent geopolitical examples include Great Britain's rise in power, eighteen centuries later, after the

Seven Years' War (1756–1763) and its victory over France[25], the rise of the United States after the First World War and of China since 1980, and Russia's current *anschluss* of Ukraine. Each time, a new power emerges, seemingly dominant beliefs are swept away, and history changes direction, making room for unexpected innovations.

The Pax Romana allowed an entire secure logistics system to emerge. Ships had access to ports, while people, armies and goods could circulate via the Roman roads. This favoured the circulation of ideas throughout the Empire, which stretched as far as Gaul at the same time[26]. Nonetheless, missionaries' journeys were long and fraught with climate uncertainties, especially at sea. In the words of Paul the Apostle, circa 55–57, "[...] three times I was shipwrecked; a night and a day I have been in the deep; in journeyings often, in perils of waters, in perils of robbers, in perils by mine own countrymen, in perils by the heathen, in perils in the city, in perils in the wilderness, in perils in the sea, in perils among false brethren" (2 Cor. 11:25–26).

Meanwhile, there appears to have been two hundred years of political instability in Judea. This combination of uncertainty and ideological tension under Roman domination created an ideal context for the emergence of religious prophets, saviours and political messiahs, of whom Jesus and then Paul the Apostle were the most prominent examples. On top of the apocalyptic imaginary of a catastrophe to come, a messianic ("populist") imaginary promising a better world was superimposed.

The term "populist" is used here in a neutral sense to describe one of the possible forms of political action, namely when political leaders invoke the difficulties of the disadvantaged social classes in an apocalyptic manner in order to come to power, as Raphael Doan explains about Julius Caesar (100–44 BC)[27], for example.

Periods of uncertainty are particularly conducive to apocalyptic and anxiety-inducing discourse[28], whose modern forms are conspiracy theories and collapsology, as seen with QAnon or the documentary *Hold-up*. The controversy surrounding chloroquine was reinterpreted in a conspiracy mode during the COVID-19 pandemic, despite the fact that quinine had already been shown to be ineffective in treating the so-called "Spanish" flu[29] back in 1918.

The function of apocalyptic and messianic imaginaries is to enchant the world, either negatively or positively, and give meaning to an historic moment when everything seems uncertain. Had there not been a strong imaginary to support it as it "took-off" from its context of origin towards its polytheistic context of adoption, the monotheistic invention would have had less chance of becoming a disruptive innovation.

*

The Temple's reach was growing, Alexandria and Antioch's Jewish communities were prospering, and the Jewish world was expanding—unless this entire dynamic were to be disrupted by an unforeseen event. This "black swan[30]" would be the Zealots' revolt and the destruction of the Second Temple in the year 70 AD.

The black-swan metaphor means that the fact that nine white swans have been observed does not mean that the tenth will not be black, something Karl Popper had already shown in the 1930s. For Nassim Nicholas Taleb, the black swan symbolizes the unpredictable in the midst of a long and seemingly eternal series. British philosopher Bertrand Russel (1872–1970) used another animal in his critique of this inductive approach: the Thanksgiving turkey. Having been fed by humans for several months, the turkey concluded, after this long series, that humans were good. Unfortunately, on the eve of a dark day called Thanksgiving, it discovered all too late that the humans were to chop off its head. The series the turkey observed may have been long, but the unforeseen black swan still arrived.

In human sciences, qualitative research allows us to approach the question of induction differently. In my practice as an anthropologist, it is a method of observation that seeks out the diversity of occurrences as well as unexpected weak signals, without ever looking for frequency or a long series. The search for invariants does not look at frequency but at systems, where each element may be an invariant, but with infinitely variable combinations. Rather like cholesterol, there is bad induction (of badly reasoned series) and good induction, which reasons in terms of a system of actions or objects.

The variation in combinations is itself the result of the interplay of actors, which can disturb any predictions a futurist might make, irrespective of whether they are based on inspecting the entrails of birds as in the past or on statistical modelling today. Both cases are socially useful because they help us make decisions, but the bases for these decisions are just as uncertain as with inductive methods. This type of research allows us to identify the invariant elements that are regularly present in innovation processes, while also recognizing that the way in which they combine in any given historical period is relatively unpredictable.

The Jewish world was no longer limited to Palestine. It stretched from the East to the West. It was as much Aramaic as Greek, oral as written. "Judaism was diverse before 70 AD[31]." Synagogues appear to have emerged in approximately the second century BC, around the Mediterranean ports such as Alexandria, Carthage, Ostia (near Rome) and Athens, but also in Asia Minor, in Byzantium (which would become Constantinople then Istanbul)[32], and along the Tigris and Euphrates around Babylon (south of present-day Baghdad). To simplify, synagogue-centred Judaism was in Greek in the west and in Aramaic in the east[33].

The Jewish, Greek and Roman worlds were already strongly intermingled. Everything was in place for Judaism to grow stronger throughout the Mediterranean. However, just because the logistical, climatic, linguistic and cultural elements are present does not mean that their combination will inevitably lead to the spread of Jewish monotheism. In addition to these elements and the innovation, the interplay of actors and unforeseen events will act either for or against the Jewish proselytizing that lies at the heart of the innovation process.

~ ~ ~

Chapter 5

The Incremental Invention Launched by Jesus: Purifying the Temple Religion

Jesus, who would become Jesus Christ after his death, had only a brief public life. It lasted two to three years, in the 30s of the common era. Little is known about his life from a historical point of view. It was part of a social and historical process that was already underway in Judea, Galilee, Samaria and the Mediterranean world, which was replete with controversies and tensions: between the Sadducee priests and the Pharisees for example, but also asceticism movements, such as the Essenes, and political-messianic movements such as the Zealots and the Sicarii. Other movements, such as the Samaritan Jews, were located between Judea in the south and Galilee in the north. The history of daily and religious life in the Jewish world is better known. Hence, historical sources on daily life in Judea are as useful for reconstructing the "earthly" life of the historical figure Jesus as the traces found in the four Gospels. The history of Jesus blends with that of the Jewish world of his time and its many religious and political currents.

The Dead Sea Scrolls, Testament to Judaism's Diversity

As Didier Long writes, archaeological discoveries, including the Qumran Caves Scrolls in 1947, reveal "another Judaism at the dawn of the common era, when Jesus and his disciples lived, a singularly more diverse and complicated Judaism than medieval and modern rabbinic Judaism would have us believe[1]". All these movements, with their blurred boundaries, represent religious inventions seeking to purify traditional religion. Some sought to spread only within Palestine, some targeted the Jewish diaspora, while others were ready to break out of the borders of the Jewish world. This society was in the grip of political and religious tumult, caught between defending the local and embracing a global form of proselytism. Until the 2000s, there was intense debate about the scrolls and fragments of Jewish religious texts found all around the Dead Sea, from Masada to the south, Qumran to the east of Jerusalem, and also Jericho a little further north, as well as in other caves. When they were discovered, they were attributed to the Essenes, an ascetic Jewish sect said to have written or copied the eight hundred scrolls found. Today, this theory seems unlikely, given how small the site is. It would have required several dozen, or even several hundred scribes to perform such a task.

The most plausible hypothesis, for the moment—and the one put forward by Norman Golb when he was a professor of Jewish history and culture at the University of Chicago—is that the Dead Sea Scrolls come from the Temple in Jerusalem. They are Jewish cultural capital of great importance, extending far beyond the Essenes at Qumran, of whom there were few (about 4,000 in all of Palestine). The scrolls were placed in the caves for their protection in the late 60s AD, a time when the Temple was at even greater risk as a result of the Zealots' religious and political revolt against the Roman occupation. Because the Roman reconquest began in Galilee to the north, the Temple staff had time to flee with the scrolls before the Temple was destroyed in 70 AD.

Qumran is more likely to have been a military fortress and not a monastery, as Father Roland de Vaux, the director of the École Biblique et Archéologique Francaise de Jérusalem and leading Qumran specialist, originally argued. According to Norman Golb, the fortress served "to guard the route carrying salt, balsam, asphalt and sugar from the Dead Sea region to the capital". From there, "the cargoes could be transferred to camelback for the rest of the journey to Jerusalem[2]" by following the wadis or dry river beds that led all the way to the city. The Temple scrolls were taken along the same route in the opposite direction for their protection.

There is however one Qumran text that can be attributed with some certainty to the Essenes, the *Community Rule*, which contains a passage from Isaiah (40:3): "A voice calls out in the wilderness, clear ye the way of the Lord[3]". This text was reprised by John the Baptist, who baptized Jesus in the River Jordan at the start of his public life in the late 30s AD. The *Community Rule* accounts for the theory that there may have been a connection between Jesus, John the Baptist and the Essenes. In any case, it raises the question of the continuity or discontinuity between Jewish purification rituals and what would later become Christian baptism. At this point though, Christianity did not exist but Israel was awash with different and often conflicting religious currents.

Judaism's Diverse Currents and Tensions Over the Interpretation of the Torah

Romano-Jewish historian Flavius Josephus (37–100) was a key witness to the first-century-AD *Jewish War* against the Romans. Although some of his religious categorizations are now being revisited and must be followed with discernment, his work suggests that the Jewish religion encompassed four main religious currents. He describes them as *haíresis* [αἵρεσις, meaning a "choice" in Ancient Greek[4]], the origin of the word "heresy[5]", which originally referred to a school of thought[6] and only became pejorative later as the norms of "true faith" crystallized. This means that at the time of Jesus, there was strong competition in the religious inventions market or the "market of souls[7]".

The Sadducees were the first current. They were close to the Temple priests and did not believe in the resurrection of the dead, nor in eternal life, nor that destiny was imposed by God. They "denied any pre-destination and maintained that God had made man the absolute master of his actions, with complete freedom of action[8]".

There are traces of this in the Gospel of Mark (12:18–27), which describes an episode of verbal jousting between Jesus and the Sadducees, engaged in a sort of forerunner to "Pilpul", a Jewish rhetorical practice for resolving contradictions, thought to have originated in sixteenth-century Poland. A woman was married to a man who had seven brothers. The man dies, and she marries his second brother, who also dies. This continues on until the seventh brother. In an effort to unnerve Jesus, the Sadducees ask him: once everyone is resurrected, whose wife will this woman be? Jesus replies that, "when they shall rise from the dead, they neither marry, nor are given in marriage; but are as the angels which are in heaven".

This exchange confirms that the matter of resurrection—whether interpreted literally or symbolically—clearly already existed in the Jewish religion, as we saw with the story of the Maccabees. The first Book of Kings, which is meant to be set in the ninth century BC, already recounts forms of resurrection. The prophet Elijah (born c. 927 BC) revives a widow's dead son (1 Kings 17:17–24) and is himself lifted up to heaven by a whirlwind (2 Kings 2:11), much like the Ascension of Jesus nine centuries later. The Book of Daniel, written in the second century BC at the same time as the Books of Maccabees, also speaks of resurrection: "But you, go your way till the end; for you shall rest, and will arise to your inheritance at the end of the days" (Dan. 12:13).

As for the anthropological answer, it would be quite simple. In "heaven", she would be the first brother's wife, because the others, as her "brothers-in-law (*levir*)[9]", were merely substitute husbands[10] taken in a levirate marriage (Deut. 25:5). The Sadducees were based at the Temple in Jerusalem. They belonged to the ruling class and were allies of the Romans, as we have seen above. They disappeared when the Temple ended.

The second current, the Zealots, was a more violent messianic movement, which took power in Jerusalem in 67 AD and eradicated the privileged and the "impure Jews" allied with the Romans. This revolt led to the the disappearance of the Temple, destroyed by emperor Titus in 70 AD, and of the priestly caste, opening the way for Judaism to spread throughout the eastern and western Mediterranean.

The Zealot movement originated in Galilee, like Jesus and like the future rabbinic movement that emerged "in the second half of the second century, after the Jews' expulsion from Judea following the failed Bar Kokhba revolt". This means that Judeo-Christianity "was born in a well-defined environment which was socially and politically marginal[11]".

This marginality is an important historical observation, because innovation rarely originates from within an institution. It often starts on the periphery of large organizations, in what today we would call a start-up[12]. Transgression is easier there, and the enthusiasm of a team of pioneers ready to work relentlessly helps overcome the difficulties and obstacles inherent in launching a new idea. Faith moves mountains (see Mark 11:23).

Again according to Josephus, a third movement with a strong popular base predominated in Galilee, to the north of Judea: the Pharisees. They believed in eternal life, like Jesus and later Paul the Apostle. We must not forget that the Gospels were written between forty and seventy years after the death of Jesus, at a time when the Judeo-Christians and the Pauline and Hellenistic Christian Jews, who followed Paul the

Apostle, were in conflict with the rabbinic Judaism that was forming in the 80s and 90s around the prominent rabbi Gamaliel II. Thus, in all the criticism against the Pharisees, it is often difficult to distinguish between what actually came from Jesus prior to the 30s and what came from this period, between 70 and 100, the time of the emergence of what would become Christianity by the middle of the second century.

The Essenes were a fourth, more ascetic movement that embraced an extreme ideal of purity. John the Baptist, who appears in the Gospel of Matthew (Matt. 3:1-7), may be partly linked to this movement. For Étienne Nodet, "John is clearly related to the Essenes" while also differentiated from them[13]. He announced the Messiah's arrival and preached purification through baptism (John 1:26). As we have seen, he baptizes Jesus in the River Jordan as he begins his public life and preaching in Galilee, a land with a particularly strong Zealot presence[14].

The Baptism of Converts: Invented by the Essenes

Untangling the baptism debate is tricky. The Jewish religion has traditional rites of purification by water, as evidenced by the *mikveh*, a small ritual pool that may be near the synagogue or in a house. As the Qumran-scrolls specialist Norman Golb writes: *"all* practicing Jews of the Roman period bathed ritually in consonance with biblical laws[15]". Hence it would seem that there is continuity between Judaism and Christianity.

But Christianity innovated with its proselyte baptism, which was "totally unknown to other branches of official Judaism of that time[16]." This inclusion of gentiles in the practices creates a discontinuity between Jewish purification rites and Christian baptism.

We can now see how, by the end of the first century AD, this ritual of purification by water, combined with the removal of circumcision, solved the problem of the uncircumciseds' impurity and their relationship with the circumcised, allowing the shift from Jewish monotheism to Christian monotheism across a much broader swathe of society. It lowers the "mental load" on the "end users", reduces the anxiety of being unclean and simplifies rituals.

From a theological standpoint, the question of baptism is extremely technical. While I may not have grasped all the nuances, I have understood, as Étienne Nodet shows, that the baptism of converts became a key component in the process of spreading Christianity in pagan contexts. The baptism of the Hellenistic Christian Jews, which meant that "the pure is stronger than the impure, opened up new avenues to foreign lands[17]". Through baptism, the very strict rules regulating what was pure or impure could be circumvented, along with the ritual purification practices of Judaism[18].

We can suppose then that because these purification rules were extremely restrictive, they inhibited the spread of Judaism. It is as if what would become Christian baptism released non-Jewish believers from the numerous purification rituals, simplifying entry into this as-yet unnamed religion of Christianity.

In the eighth book of his *Rabbi's Cat* series, Joann Sfar gives us a comical description of the issue through the voice of a young rabbi who refuses to convert a young woman to Judaism:

> If you had told me: "I don't know what's happening to me, I just love your ceremonies and your commandments. Apparently there are 613 of them? Ah, I can't wait to learn them all and scrupulously apply them, for with all my heart I love only God and I fear only God" ... Well, if you'd told me that, I would have probably sent you to a psychiatrist because it's beyond me why anyone would want a religion as restrictive as mine.[19]

By simplifying Judaism's rules on purification, at least for the most rigorous practices, Christian baptism delivers one of the great constants of all successful inventions: they simplify life, they "reduce the mental load". They also reduce, at least potentially, the guilt that comes with not following the rules.

Reducing constraints is an important invariant of innovation processes. These constraints determine the chances of the innovation spreading. An "incoming innovation"[20], which is the entry phase of a new technique, service or belief into a different or foreign environment, has little chance of spreading if it is too complicated to use, if the norm among the receiving group is not in favour, if the time it takes to learn (and therefore to convert) is too long, if there are too many gauge changes and transshipments from one place to another in the logistics process, if the budget, tithe or tax cost is too high, or if there are no social networks to transfer it from one environment to another.

Without a "transferor", to borrow a concept from the sociologist Gaétan Brisepierre on the green and energy transition, there is no diffusion[21]. Here, we can understand the debate among the different currents of Judaism on the strict application of the "Law of Moses" in the first century AD as a strategic issue for actors with constraints, some of whom support the limited diffusion of the monotheistic invention and others a more widespread one. Expanding the market of ideas requires lowering the mental load associated with adopting monotheism, which Christianity did by simplifying the rituals, unlike Judaism.

The Historical Jewish Dimension of Jesus' Life

Jesus spent his entire childhood and youth in Galilee. He was raised in an orthodox Jewish world, as evidenced by his circumcision, his "bar mitzvah", his religious practices and his travelling to Jerusalem for Passover. According to Didier Long, he may even have belonged to a popular pious movement in Galilee, the Hasidim, which was itself part of the wider Pharisee movement[22].

In reality, it is very difficult to clearly categorize Jesus' religious affiliation within the Jewish religion. In his opposition to the Sadducees, he was aligned with the Pharisees, themselves a heterogeneous group that comprised a "traditionalist" current and a "liberal" current. On the other hand, Jesus opposed them on the importance of oral traditions, which the Pharisees held dear. This is why Étienne Nodet and Justin Taylor believe Jesus cannot be strictly considered a Pharisee[23].

He may also have been close to the Messianic Zealots, a group that originated in Galilee[24]: "Zealots and Pharisees may have been violently opposed on the ground, but [...] they were very close in fundamental ideas and customs[25]". For the two authors, "[Jesus] was certainly not a Sadducee, since there were none in Galilee and they denied the resurrection and divine providence [or predestination]. Nor was he a Pharisee, since he extolled Scripture in opposition to the ancestral customs. And he was not an Essene, despite his advocacy of baptism and Scripture, since he insisted on coming to Jerusalem and accepted the Temple as it was. Finally, he was not really a zealot, even though his movement caused the politicians some anxieties[26]".

Depending on the debate, his religious identity can be linked to the Pharisees, the Essenes or the Zealots, but not the Sadducees. Jesus' social relationships, and especially his apostles, reflect Galilee's diversity, because the Gospels show that he had ties with Zealots, former disciples of John the Baptist, a tax collector and Pharisees[27].

The preaching of Jesus found in the Gospels is all in continuity and imbued with the Jewish Torah. All of this has been recognized by historians today and is less controversial. One significant example of this continuity is the text of the Lord's Prayer (Matt. 6:7–13)[28]. The first part is directly inspired by one of the most important prayers of the Jewish liturgy, the Kaddish, which is recited after a death, as a mourning ritual, though not exclusively so, because it is first and foremost a prayer of praise to God[29]. The Lord's Prayer is also inspired by the morning and evening prayer, the Shema Yisrael, "Hear, O Israel". In the Gospel of Matthew (Matt. 5:17), Jesus confirms this continuity between his teaching and the Torah: "Do not think that I came to destroy the Law or the Prophets. I did not come to destroy but to fulfill."

This influence is frequently found in the words of Jesus, such as in the Beatitudes in the Gospels of Matthew and Luke. Didier Long recalls that already in Psalm 37, we read that "the meek shall inherit the earth" (Ps. 37:11), i.e. the kingdom of God. Jesus said: "Blessed are you poor, for yours is the kingdom of God" (Luke 6:20). The statements in the Beatitudes are largely inspired by the Jewish tradition.[30]

Similarly, a common process with the Gospels is to go looking in the Torah for elements that prove the continuity between the discourse of Jesus and his predecessors. For example, in the Gospel according to Saint Matthew, Jesus says: "Foxes have holes and birds of the air have nests" (Matt. 8:20). This verse is a reference to Psalm 84, which probably dates from the sixth century BC, where it is written that "even the sparrow has found a home, and the swallow a nest for herself, where she may lay her young". As Didier Long shows, the argument does not seek to demonstrate a historical reality, but a spiritual continuity.

Because the Gospels, like the parables, use metaphor, it can be difficult to distinguish between what belonged, in the first century AD, to the Jewish tradition or to the future Christian tradition.

Many of these parables, these stories announcing the coming of the Messiah and the rewards or punishments associated with his return, reflect the practices of Galilee's agrarian society. They speak of wheat, weeds, farmers, fig trees and of oil for lamps. Parables often end with a moral like this one: "Watch therefore, for you know neither the day nor the hour" (implied: of the Messiah's return) (Mat. 25:13).

While the Gospels reprise many Jewish themes, from the resurrection of the dead to the coming of the Messiah, "God's presence (*shekhina*) in this world in the form of the spirit and his wisdom [...], the sharing of wine and bread [during the *Seder* meal, the future Christian Eucharist], baptism[31]", there is also the Christian innovation, namely the baptism of non-Jewish converts[32]. The Holy Spirit exists in the Jewish tradition. It represents the power of God among men. It is not independent from God. The debate on the Trinity, the concept of one God in three persons, Father, Son and Holy Spirit, emerged from this tradition and was only settled three hundred years later, at the Council of Nicaea (325 AD).

Some Protestant traditions diverge from the Catholic tradition and reinterpret the resurrection as a symbolic event. In 1926, Rudolf Bultmann showed that Jesus' death and resurrection must be interpreted symbolically, as a reinterpretation done by the Judeo-Greek community in the first centuries of the common era[33]. In the First Epistle to the Corinthians, the apostle Paul says: "And if Christ is not risen, then our preaching is empty and your faith is also empty" (1 Co. 15:14), but he later adds: "It is sown a natural body, it is raised a spiritual body" (1 Co. 15:44). This can be interpreted as symbolic resurrection of the dead, similar to Jesus' answer to the Sadducees.

According to the Acts of the Apostles and the Gospels written around 80–90 AD, after his death, Jesus appeared to his apostles for forty days. On Ascension Day, his apostles asked him: "Lord, will You at this time restore the kingdom to Israel?" He answered: "It is not for you to know times or seasons which the Father has put in His own authority" (Acts 1:6–7).

By the time the Acts of the Apostles were put into writing, Jesus had been dead for over fifty years and still had not returned. So, how to deal with this cognitive dissonance between the belief in the Messiah's return and the non-return thereof? The role of managing this dissonance fell especially to the most important "mobilizing figure"[34] in the spread of the Christian Jewish innovation, Paul the Apostle.

Jesus, an Inventor Hesitating Between Reform and Revolution

There is no absolute break between the preaching's of Jesus and the various Jewish religious currents, including the messianic-apocalyptic tradition, also found in the words of John the Evangelist. The preaching of Jesus is embedded in the political and religious conflicts rocking

Judea, Galilee and Samaria. As Didier Long writes: "Nothing in the birth certificate of Christianity suggested that it would one day constitute a separate religion from Judaism[35]". The innovation would come later, and still in a fragile way, with Paul the Apostle.

For Didier Long, Jesus cannot be the creator of Christianity in the modern sense of the term, even if he does appear to have been the inventor who first inspired Paul the Apostle and then the Hellenistic Christian Jews. An autonomous Christian group is unlikely to have existed in the Jewish world before the second half of the second century[36]. Prior to this period, there was great uncertainty as to which Jewish current would lead to Christianity.

This uncertainty is present whenever most innovations are launched, then as now. Using the principle of symmetry, if we analyze both successful and unsuccessful inventions, we understand that Jesus' ideas could very well have disappeared, much like the Judeo-Christians in the strict sense, i.e. those who followed James the Just, the brother of Jesus. Some of his ideas were probably also incorporated into what would become rabbinic Judaism after the destruction of the Temple.

For the time being, we have an inventor—Jesus—but in the midst of other religious movements. His words will be taken up later and reinterpreted according to the different Christian currents. Jesus' objective was not to create a new religion, but above all to purify the Temple religion practised by the Hellenized Sadducees, allied with the Romans. At the same time, he belonged to the current that favoured proselytism, even if this is not always clear in the texts that quote him. He would serve as a justification for the future Christian current.

This goal of purification is illustrated in the Gospel of Matthew, in the story of the merchants driven out of the Temple:

> Then Jesus went into the temple of God and drove out all those who bought and sold in the temple, and overturned the tables of the money changers and the seats of those who sold doves. And He said to them, "It is written, *My house shall be called a house of prayer* [a reference to Isa. 56:7, where Isaiah refers to burnt offerings using the term ὁλό-χαυτος (holocaust), which in ancient Greek meant that the victim was wholly consumed]; but you have made it a *den of thieves* [a reference to Jer. 7:11]" (Matt. 21:12–13).

Seeking to purify the religious practices of the Temple is more of an incremental invention than a disruptive innovation, even if the practice is transgressive. This is why he was sentenced to death by crucifixion by the Roman governor of Judea, Pontius Pilate.

Placing the Responsibility for Jesus' Death on the Sadducees of the Sanhedrin

The historian Reza Aslan shows that, contrary to what the Gospels of Matthew and Mark recount, the Sanhedrin could not sit at night nor during the Jewish Passover or on the eve of Shabbat. Reza Aslan refers to the Mishna, a record of the oral rules of the Torah written at the time as the Gospels, forty to seventy years after Jesus died.

Hence it could not have been the Jewish high priest Caiaphas but rather Pontius Pilate who convicted Jesus, probably without a trial. Pilate was "renowned for his loathing of the Jews" and "as the histories reveal, was not one for trials. In his ten years as governor of Jerusalem, he had sent thousands upon thousands to the cross". In Reza Aslan's view, "Jesus was executed by the Roman state for the crime of sedition". For him, the historic figure of Jesus was closer to a revolutionary zealot or messiah than to a Pharisee or a "gentle shepherd"[37]. The problem was that presenting Jesus as a revolutionary who opposed Roman power made it difficult to spread his religious innovation within the Greco-Roman world, which was the goal of the Christian Jews of Greek culture and the Pagan Christians. His anti-Roman aspect had to be erased.

The "invention" of Jesus being sentenced by the Jews is a textbook example in terms of method and difficulty of historical interpretation. To understand this trial, we must not refer to the historical period when it may have taken place, but rather to the time in which the text was received. It was written at least forty years after the events, in the midsts of a battle for the spread of the innovation. The narrative of the trial mirrors the power play between on the one hand the social networks of the Hellenistic Christian Jews, who spoke Greek and distanced themselves from the Torah, and on the other hand the Judean, Galilean and Jewish Diaspora networks that followed the Torah in Hebrew. Some Jews of the Diaspora would have been torn between the Hebrew of the Torah and the Greek of the Septuagint.

It was therefore necessary to "enchant" part of the innovation's history for it to be better received by the pagans and the Greco-Roman Jews. This explains the "invention" of Jewish responsibility for the trial of Jesus in Gospel accounts. The Gospel of Mark, the oldest of the four Gospels, was written around 70 AD in Rome, far away from the original Jewish culture. Outside the legal context of Judea itself, it would have been easier to explain that the Jews organized the trial[38]. The objective at the time was to minimize Roman responsibility for Jesus' death in order to make the innovation more acceptable in the Roman pagan world. This would be called "storytelling" today.

In addition, blaming the Jews for the death of Jesus also served to disqualify a competitor—rabbinic Judaism—which had been emerging since the destruction of the temple in Jerusalem. Its monotheism was enjoying some success in the major cities around the Mediterranean rim.

However, some religious Jews would never accept someone who died on a cross as a true prophet, nor as the Messiah. Christianity (as it would later become) gained greatly by transforming Jesus of Nazareth into the resurrected Jesus Christ, thus "enchanting" his death on the Cross. Without this transformation, the Christianity invention would never have been able to spread or become one of the most important innovations in the Western world in the space of two or three centuries. One of the functions of religious inventions is to enchant reality and give it meaning.

Today, this enchantment function is provided in a non-religious way by advertizing, which is essentially part of this same imaginary process of sublimating reality. This communication technique serves to enchant the invention so as to give it meaning and a competitive edge over other inventions[39].

Advertizing can be traced back to an ancient animistic mechanism, similar to polytheism, in which objects possess either an evil or a benevolent force. The "advertizing promise", like the promised land of Canaan, offers consumers the hope of a better life or a new identity thanks to the symbolic energy transmitted by incorporating or using the product or service. It personifies the product through the creation of a brand to which one must be "loyal"[40]. In terms of the anthropological search for invariants, advertizing is indeed the equivalent of a magical practice of transubstantiation, of changing the substance of an ordinary object into a marvellous one. In a way, the diversity of brands represents a modern form of polytheism and magico-religious messaging.

On the matter of enchantment, it is worth bringing in what Daniel Marguerat, a Protestant historian, writes about miracles: "Luke [the author to who one of the four Gospels is attributed] creates a system in which words and miracles work together to produce faith [...] the miracle lends credibility to the message [...] without miracles, the words are hollow. Without words, the miracle is in danger of saying too much[41]." [Translator's note: this is a free translation from the French]. The magico-religious dimension of Judaism corresponds partly to polytheism and therefore partly to animism, in which objects have agency and divinities operate in daily life at a very practical level, as is the case with Vodun in Benin[42]. This of course is not at all pejorative. It is important to recall that polytheism was very much the norm at the time. Monotheism remained an "oddity" in the Greco-Roman world.

*

Some religious currents were opposed to the priests of the Jerusalem temple, who were accused of being "defiled by graft and enticed by lucre[43]". Jesus took part in these opposition movements. These tensions fed apocalyptic movements proclaiming the end of time, eschatological currents on life after death and resurrection, and messianic ones heralding the arrival of a messiah who would save Israel. The first century was a period of great anxiety. This is why the first Judeo-Christians lived in communities, as a way of anticipating and waiting for the coming of the Messiah to liberate the world.

All these movements contained the promise of a better world. Many subsequent socio-political movements and innovations would do the same, from Marx's classless society to Donald Trump's MAGA ("Make America Great Again"), the internet bringing freedom for all, and marketing in general with its myriad of promises. Intellectual currents such as David Graeber's "anarchist anthropology" belong to this same pattern of condemning today's world in the name of a "lost paradise" of hunters and gatherers, lost with the invention of the State between the Tigris and the Euphrates[44]. His critique of the present is based on a very detailed description of a past world that probably never existed but is presented as a paradise lost that gives meaning to the present[45]. There can be no shift towards action without enchantment, without miracle.

Likewise, there can be no shift towards action without an organizer or a logistician. In *The Art of War*, which he probably wrote in the fourth century BC, Sun Tzu already stressed the importance of logistics: "A general rule for military operations calls for a thousand chariots, a thousand leather-covered wagons, a hundred thousand armored troops, and provisions for several hundred miles". [Translator's note: the English version is taken from Sun Tzu, The Art of War. Translated by Thomas Cleary. Boston: Shambhala Dragon Editions. 1988] In analyses of innovation processes or societal changes, logistics, distribution points and the sales force are regularly forgotten in favour of ideas and "great narratives". Yet, to plagiarize Rabelais, we could say that "Great narratives without logistics are but the ruination of innovations"[46].

Innovations also need mobilizing personalities. Their function is to make the invention acceptable in other cultures, societies or social groups, using other means than the mere power of the inventor's ideas. Their function is to bring the invention into play within society, into the interplay of actors and "pre-digital" networks, so that the invention can be reinterpreted in the host culture that receives it, and the incremental invention can be transformed into a disruptive innovation. This took two and a half centuries to achieve and was the work of Paul the Apostle and then of the Church Fathers, the first authors to organize the defence of Christianity.

Irrespective of the complexity of the tensions, conflicts and alliances among the different first-century Jewish currents, we must not forget that two important movements emerged after the destruction of the Temple: rabbinic Judaism, with strong ties to Galilee[47], and the Hellenistic Jews associated with the gentiles, also called Pauline Christians or Pagan-Christians. The reason for the term "Pauline" is that as Paul the Apostle took on the task of spreading the Christian Jewish innovation among the gentiles, the pagans, he became known as "the apostle to the Gentiles". This means that in the heart of the polytheistic world, two competitors were emerging on the market for monotheistic religious innovations, that is, the market of the gods[48].

~ ~ ~

Chapter 6

Paul the Apostle on the Road to Disruptive Innovation

As historian Paul Geoltrain writes: "The preaching of both the early witnesses and their master [Jesus] remained oral, all the more so since they were awaiting his imminent return[1]". The question of the second coming of the Messiah, and thus of the liberation of the people of Israel from Roman oppression, is crucial to understanding the innovation process that would lead Christian monotheism to separate from Jewish monotheism.

Messianic Effervescence in the First Century AD

Throughout the first half of the first century, the political situation in Israel was unstable: "Galilee, where the Zealot movement originated, was in a state of unrest that heralded the first revolt [which would take place in 66][2]". The Zealots sought to "rid Judea of the occupier in order to precipitate the arrival of eschatological times[3]". This unrest was also the result of an impoverishment of the peasant population "caused by heavy taxes, on top of the Temple taxes, and the difficult farming conditions. The great famine in around the year 60 is a testimony to this. There was a huge divide between the peasants on the one hand and the landowners and priestly aristocracy on the other [...]. These tensions added to a religious atmosphere already marked by messianic and eschatological expectation[4]".

The historian Enrico Norelli counts some ten messiahs in the years 30–70. Clearly then, this was a particularly agitated period fraught with political risks. The messiahs were risking their lives. Jesus, a native of Galilee, was one of these messiahs who challenged the Temple order, but not the Torah. Members of the priestly caste tried to have him arrested by the Romans, by setting a trap for him on the very sensitive issue of taxes, which we have seen were a heavy burden on the peasants of Judea and Galilee. They ask him:

> "Is it lawful for us to give tribute unto Caesar, or no?" But He perceived their craftiness, and said to them, "Why do you test me? Show me a penny. Whose image and superscription hath it?" They answered and said, "Caesar's". And He said to them, "Render therefore unto Caesar the things which be Caesar's, and unto God the things which be God's" (Luke 20:22–25).

Jesus avoids arrested with this "politically correct" answer, only to be arrested, sentenced and executed a few months later.

Thirty-five years after his death, the Zealots' impatience and desire to accelerate the coming of the Messiah led to the destruction of the temple in Jerusalem. This in turn led to the separation of the heterodox Christian Jews from the orthodox Jews in the second century AD. In some ways, it all could have played out differently: "Jesus' mission could have died with him[5]", or "when Jesus died, his endeavour seemed to have ended in failure[6]". If the Roman Empire were a cluster of points, 90 % of them would be polytheistic and 10 % Jewish monotheistic, and Jesus would be a tiny, almost invisible dot.

The innovation could not have developed without two "mobilizing figures"[7]: Jesus' apostle Peter; and Paul the Apostle, who did not know Jesus but joined his disciples in around 33 AD. They carried change and innovation beyond Palestine. There have been a number of "mobilizing figures" like them throughout history.

They are the organizers, like Lenin for Marx or Steve Jobs for Steve Wozniak. In his book on the sociology of decision-making, Haroun Jamous describes the creation of CHU teaching hospitals in France and the role of Professor Debré as a "reforming figure". He was one of the first authors in sociology to describe the decision, and hence the invention that is the result of a whole series of decisions, as a social process. In our work, Sophie Taponier and I chose the equivalent term "mobilizing figure" because it is somewhat more neutral as regards the positive or negative quality of the change[8].

Antagonism as Israel Awaits the Messiah

After his death, the portion of the Jewish community that recognized Jesus as the Messiah left Galilee for Jerusalem, in Judea, to await his return. The Acts of the Apostles recounts the "marvellous" story of Pentecost (πεντήκοντα = fifty, in ancient Greek). The apostles gathered on the Jewish harvest festival, Shavuot, the Feast of Weeks, fifty days after Pesach, the Jewish Passover, and fifty days after the death of Jesus. On this day, the Holy Spirit descended upon the Apostles in the form of "tongues, as of fire", a symbolic bio-energy. Daniel Marguerat explains that "fire is a common metaphor in Judaism for eschatological judgement [the final judgement when the world ends][9]", which will take place once the Messiah has returned. They also received the ability to speak in tongues, allowing them to be understood in all languages (Acts 2:1–11).

The story of Pentecost symbolizes the intense messianic expectations in Judea in general and among the Judeo-Christians of Jerusalem in particular. Acts presents the apostle Peter as the leader of the group[10]. Peter is also presented as the first to have brought an uncircumcised man into the Judeo-Christian community, a centurion named Cornelius (Acts 10:1–43), even if the event itself is disputed. The purpose of this account is to relativize the traditional Jewish conception of the pure and impure, and thus allow Judaism to be opened up to the Gentiles.

Around the year 40, "James, the brother of Jesus, became the head of the Church in Jerusalem[11]". The Judeo-Christians in the strict sense of the term belonged to this current. They sought to purify the practices of the Temple and were disinclined to open up to Gentiles who did not respect kashrut and were not circumcised.

Believing that the Second Coming was imminent, some community members abandoned all their possessions: "Now all who believed were together, and had all things in common, and sold their possessions and goods, and divided them among all, as anyone had need. So continuing daily with one accord in the temple, and breaking bread from house to house" (Acts 2:44–46)[12].

This collective quasi-withdrawal from the world is not so different from the practice of certain collapsologists today. For example, Gérald Bronner recalls Michel Besson and Bernard Vidal's description of a utopian community in 1970s France in which everything was pooled, "including clothes, books, musical instruments, tools, the money that each person brought, etc.".

Among the Judeo-Christians, this was not problem-free. One couple, Ananias and Sapphira, who were probably not entirely convinced that the Messiah was coming, kept back some of their resources. By not putting all their assets in one basket, Ananias and Sapphira followed the old agrarian polytheistic practice of risk diversification that we saw earlier. In their case, things did not turn out well. Peter (Saint Peter) punished them on the spot: "[…] Ananias […] fell down and breathed his last. And the young men arose and wrapped him up, carried him out, and buried him" (Acts 5:5–6).

This period of waiting was full of antagonism: between Sadducee Jews and the Judeo-Christians around James the Just, themselves close to the Pharisees; between Judean Jews and the Galilean Jews close to the Zealots; between Judeo-Christians and Hellenistic Christian Jews, those in favour of opening up to the Gentiles and those against. Simon Claude Mimouni and Pierre Maraval identify six different currents among Jesus' disciples: there were followers of James, Peter, "Stephen's Hellenists, Barnabas' Hellenists, the Paulines and the Johannines [who followed John][13]".

Stephen, a Hellenistic Christian Jew, found himself in the midsts of a conflict between "Hellenist" Christian Jews and "Hebrew" Judeo-Christians, who were accused of slighting the widows of Hellenistic Jews. The controversy led to him being put in charge of the Hellenistic group (Acts 6:1–7). Nevertheless, there was extreme tension between him and the high priest and he was eventually cast out of Jerusalem and stoned to death (Acts 7:55–60). All of these rather violent incidents are a good reflection of the tense atmosphere of the time, as we can reconstruct it from the fragments of stories that have reached us.

This type of human behaviour is all very normal, not morally speaking but anthropologically so. The constant existence of tensions between humans should give pause to the *laudator temporis acti*, these praisers of times past, who have always tended to enchant the good old days, as Lucien Jerphagnon shows[14]. Even Cicero (106–43 BC) said: "*O tempora! O mores!*" (Oh the times! Oh the customs!), which could be very loosely translated as: "It's all going to the dogs".

Returning to our extended metaphor, one could say that this conflictual atmosphere is not so far removed from what can occur between research and development, finance, production and marketing divisions in today's large organizations. This is especially true when they are subject to strong pressure from more-competitive Chinese prices on the international market, something I have observed in various studies I carried out in industrial companies post 2008.

For Daniel Marguerat, who is a specialist in the analysis of the Acts of the Apostles, "the core conflict is the revelation that with the risen Jesus, the holiness of Israel is extended to every man and woman who believes[15]". The Acts of the Apostles was written by Luke, presumed to have been close to Paul, in the 80s, at a time when Judaism's survival was severely threatened by the destruction of the Temple and the enslavement of a section of the Judeans. He "has in mind a universal [...] Christianity breaking with the exclusivism of Israel[16]".

To extend or not to extend Judaism to non-Jews, that is the question. For those Jews who followed Jesus, proselytism was thus perceived as a life-and-death issue. Jesus would serve as a justification for extending Judaism beyond the Jewish world, thereby ensuring its survival, but in a new form. Judaism would be reinterpreted by the Greco-Roman host environment, resulting in Christianity.

James and the Judeo-Christian Strategy of Religious Exclusivism

Applying kashrut (the rules on prohibited foods) and circumcision to gentiles—or *goyim*, meaning foreigners in Hebrew—was a highly controversial topic among Jews in general and in particular the Christian Jews aligned with Jesus. They formed the early Judeo-Christian community in Jerusalem and were led by James the Just, brother of Jesus[17].

We should note here that in the Catholic tradition, Jesus had no brothers born of "the same father and mother", as they say in the Congo. One long-standing theory invoked by Etienne Nodet and Julien Taylor is that James was the son of "Joseph, but not of Mary", as he "could be the issue of a previous marriage[18]". In the Protestant tradition, and for historians such as Pierre-Antoine Bernheim and Enrico Norelli[19], James was the brother of Jesus. That would have made him a descendant of King David, like Jesus, and given him a form of pre-eminence over the other apostles, even over Peter, if we follow the Gospel of Thomas and the Gospel of the Hebrews quoted by Pierre-Antoine Bernheim[20]. Even if these two Gospels are considered apocryphal in the Catholic tradition, they still provide valuable accounts of the time from a historical perspective.

James' objective was in line with that of Jesus: to reform the Jewish religion. James is said to have been a *nazir*, i.e. a pure Jew, a term which, according to Didier Long, is the origin of the term Nazarene. He spread Jesus' message after his death and advocated a strict Judaism that applied the Torah. According to Pierre-Antoine Bernheim, "James opposed Paul and his message that implied a redefinition of Israel's identity and of the role of the Law. Paul envisaged a unified community of Jews and Gentiles that transcended traditional borders and the specificity of Judaism. James deemed this concept unacceptable[21]".

From the perspective of strategic anthropology, this is not just a debate about doctrine. It indicates the desire of a part of the Jewish population to expand, as shown by the size of the Jewish diaspora around the Mediterranean. The debate is also the expression of the sense of threat hanging over the Jewish people since the disappearance of the Temple. The fear of disappearing triggers a choice between defensive withdrawal or strategic expansion.

From this perspective, the debate over doctrine is analyzed as a justification narrative to support the chosen strategy of one or other of the currents of Judaism, one of which has aligned with Jesus. Seen from this angle, no one narrative is truer than the others. On the other hand, the narrative allows us to understand which strategy is the most effective and who will win or lose in this competition between Jewish monotheism, the future Christian monotheism and Greco-Roman polytheisms.

James was condemned by the Sadducean priestly caste shortly before the year 70. His death was truly traumatic for the Judeo-Christian community in Jerusalem. The figure of the rabbi emerged between the first and second centuries AD. One faction thought to have emerged from this Judeo-Christian group are the Ebionites, of whom traces have been found at Pella, a city on the other side of the River Jordan in present-day Jordan. Descendants of the Ebionite Christians may have had contact with Muhammad in the seventh century: "A direct influence between Ebionite Judeo-Christianity and early Islam would appear to be conceivable[22]".

James' death probably facilitated the development process of the Christian Jewish innovation, because James advocated traditional rules more than the new rules proposed by Paul. Peter was on the fence.

To continue relating all of this to modern examples, the fall of the Judeo-Christians is akin to the fate of the Minitel, which was developed by French engineers in the 1980s and succumbed to the global expansion of the world wide web[23].

It all could have ended there had it not been for Paul the Apostle converting the "gentiles", many of whom were of Greco-Roman culture, and Peter developing the Christian Jewish current among the Hellenistic Jews beyond Judea. Peter is often referred to in the canonical texts as the apostle of the circumcised and Paul as the apostle of the uncircumcised around the Mediterranean rim and as far as the two historic rivers Tigris and Euphrates: "[...] the gospel for the uncircumcised had been committed to me, as the gospel for the circumcised was to Peter", writes Paul in the Epistle to the Galatians (Galatia was north of present-day Turkey) (Gal. 2:7).

Eliminating Circumcision Opens Up the New Religious Market of the Gentiles

In the Catholic tradition, Peter is considered the first pope and therefore the successor of Jesus. This was also a matter of disagreement between the different currents of Christianity. Historically, the centralization of religious power took place at least a hundred years after Peter's death. At the outset, the Christian Jews were a network of communities with bishops or "presbyters" (elders) leading religious communities with no centralized power[24]. They governed in a collegiate manner. This network mirrored the network of cities that lay all around the Mediterranean. Collegiality disappeared in the second century to be replaced by a single bishop in Rome[25].

According to the Acts of the Apostles (Acts 22:3), Paul studied under a very famous "liberal" Pharisee named Gamaliel, the father of Gamaliel II who would launch rabbinic Judaism. Shortly after joining the Jewish current that recognized Jesus as the Messiah in the 30s, Paul was in Jerusalem where he was brought before the Sanhedrin, which was composed of Sadducees, who did not believe in the resurrection of the dead, and Pharisees who did. During his trial, Paul appealed to the latter for their support, saying: "Men and brethren, I am a Pharisee, the son of a Pharisee; concerning the hope and resurrection of the dead I am being judged!" (Acts 23:6). In so doing, Paul invokes his origins in the Jewish Pharisaic tradition on which he would rely to transform Jesus, the Messiah and prophet, into Christ, the risen King.

The resurrection he is defending is symbolic. It is similar to the different forms of resurrection found in the Torah. It is compatible with Platonism, which prevailed in the Roman world and valued ideas over the body and matter, and hence able to be received outside the Judean world. This debate would continue for several centuries. There would be endless disputes over whether Jesus was only a man, only a god or an image of God, a man and a god, or a God in three persons, and in what form he rose from the dead. All of this was not settled, at least temporarily, until the Council of Nicaea in the fourth century, two hundred and fifty years later.

Paul was to play the role of translator, of mediator, between Hebrew and Greek culture. "[He] spoke in Hebrew for liturgical prayer, study and for reading the Torah in the synagogue, in Aramaic when addressing his compatriots, and he wrote his letters or epistles between 50 and 60 in Greek[26]". He thus played a central role as a linguistic and religious interface with a new Mediterranean and Middle Eastern population. He opened up a whole new field of development for the religious innovation which, from the end of the first century and throughout the second century AD, had fewer and fewer ties to the Aramaic-speaking Judean world and was increasingly in Greek.

Paul the Apostle favoured not applying circumcision and dietary rules to the gentiles (*gentiles*, or "pagans", in Latin), whereas Peter was more hesitant. This difference over the development strategy for the "new service" sparked a conflict in Antioch (present-day Antakya in southern Turkey) in the 50s between the circumcised Jews close to James and the equally circumcised Hellenistic Jews. During a mission to Antioch, where Paul shared his meals with the Gentiles, Peter on the other hand refused to eat with those who were not circumcised and did not practice kashrut. This angered Paul, who criticized Peter publicly: "[...] before certain men came from James, he would eat with the Gentiles; but when they came, he withdrew and separated himself, fearing those who were of the circumcision" (Gal. 2:11–13).

Peter seemed to have had difficulty making clear-cut decisions. He even seems to have been rather fearful, if we believe the account in the Gospel of Luke—which probably reflects Paul's thinking—of Peter's denial after Jesus was arrested on the eve of his death (Luke 22:54–62).

A little later, a meeting with James in Jerusalem decided to settle the matter in Paul's favour, accepting an accommodation on circumcision while maintaining basic dietary rules: "[...] we should not trouble those from among the Gentiles who are turning to God" (Acts 15:19). They are simply asked to abstain from food offered to idols and from blood and the meat of strangled animals, but are seemingly not required to be circumcised. This first compromise allowed the Christian Jewish invention to develop. In relaxing these rules for non-Jews, reference is made to the time of Noah, who lived before they were revealed to Moses and was therefore not circumcised. This ensured that these major rules of the Torah were not lifted for the Jews. Making the conversion process less stringent created a grey area that allowed the innovation to spread more easily. Thanks to Paul, the mobilizing figure in the innovation's spread, a major barrier was being torn down.

The Cognitive Dissonance of Messianic Disillusionment Leads to Proselytism

The Messiah did not return. Disillusioned, some members left the community. The others found a way to end the cognitive dissonance created by the gap between the fantasy of the Messiah's return and the reality of his non-return. Paradoxically, their solution was to step up their proselytism (προσήλυτος, which in ancient Greek originally referred to a newcomer in a country)[27].

This mechanism was explained two thousand years later by Leon Festinger and his colleagues in their book *When Prophecy Fails*[28]. In the *Corpus Christi* series on the television channel Arte, Daniel Marguerat points out that a link can be made between this 1956 sociological study and the let-down of the non-return of the Messiah in the first century AD.

Leon Festinger's study describes a group in Michigan, USA, in the Great Lakes region, who believed that a "great flood was due to engulf the city at dawn on December 21 [in the 1950s], but the believers thought that they would be rescued before the cataclysm took place.

They expected flying saucers to land, pick up the chosen ones, and transport them either to other planets or to some 'safe places' designated by the Guardians". But the flying saucers never came, although they had been announced on several occasions, and there was no flood. Festinger described the immense disappointment created each time they did not appear as "cognitive dissonance", being the gap between expectations and what actually occurs.

One example of cognitive dissonance, but in this case without proselytizing, can be found in *The Fox and the Grapes*, which La Fontaine adapted from one of Aesop's fables. The fox wants to eat some grapes, but when he realises they are too high to reach, he says they are unripe, thus resolving the cognitive dissonance between his desire and his ability to satisfy it. The original version of this fable dates from the sixth century BC and Aesop would have written it in Greek. The Greco-Latin origin of the fable confirms that cognitive dissonance is an ancient mechanism and therefore a human invariant.

This inner discordance creates intense psychological tension. The subject will try to mitigate it by either abandoning the belief and returning to reality, withdrawing into a small community of believers, or conversely attempting to spread the belief by becoming a proselytizer and practising the "art of *intéressement* [the art of interesting an increasing number of allies][29]". Increasing the number of believers helps the subject deal with the dissonance, which tends to disappear thanks to the feeling of belonging to a very large group of people[30]: "Proselyting, after all, is not the sole means by which support for a belief system can be won[31]". The unmet "messianic expectation" can be offset by searching for signs, miracles, and "supernatural" events. Proselytizing reduces the suffering caused by the confronting gaps between reality, social constraints and the aspirations of the various actors interacting in society.

I was very struck by the similarities between the Pentecost story, which marks the beginning of Christian Jewish proselytism, and the Michigan community's story: the Biblical Flood and the one they awaited; Noah's ark and the flying saucers; the expectation of the Messiah and of aliens; and lastly, proselytism. So much so that I wondered whether the biblical scenario and the one in Acts could have implicitly served as a "cultural repertoire", as models for managing belief and messianic cognitive dissonance in America.

American Trumpism, Another Example of Cognitive Dissonance

We can also make a connection with more-recent US events. In January 2021, 72 % of Republicans were "still attributing President Biden's victory to voter fraud[32]". They believed that Donald Trump had the ability to assert his rights and return to power, like a new messiah. It was this belief, which was partly organized[33], that was behind the violent assault on the Capitol on January 6th 2021, an attack that evokes the story of the apostle Peter who drew his sword to defend Jesus when he was arrested on the Mount of Olives near Jerusalem (John 18:10).

The assault on the Capitol, and thus on the federal government, is associated with an invisible "deep state", the equivalent of the Roman Empire. This anti-state belief has a distinctly American libertarian foundation, of which one of the most famous figures is the Russian-born philosopher and novelist Ayn Rand.

In her novel *Atlas Shrugged*, she wrote: "I'm [...] the man who robs the thieving poor and gives back to the productive rich [...] Robin Hood [...] is the man who became the symbol of the idea that need, not achievement, is the source of rights[34]". I am not sure that there is an equivalent movement to this in France, because the heroes of her libertarian novel are entrepreneurs who want to create a paradise with no state. Her rejection of the state could bring her closer culturally but not ideologically to the anarchist anthropology mentioned above. This novel is allegedly one of the most influential books in the United States after the Bible.

The urban revolt led by paramilitary groups such as the Proud Boys, the Oath Keepers[35] and the Boogaloo[36], an American apocalyptic movement whose practices are equivalent to those of the Zealots, ended in a huge disappointment. Just as Jesus did not oppose his own arrest, Trump did not come inside the Capitol with them, despite saying live on CNN on January 6th 2021: *"I'll be there with you"*, a phrase with Christian overtones evocative of Jesus saying "I am with you always, even unto the end of the world" (Mat. 28:20).

They were left to deal with the cognitive dissonance between their expectation of Donald Trump's victory over the federal state and a reality that falls far short of it. The dissonance would grow even more in the aftermath when some leaders were indicted by the FBI[37]. This would all appear to jeopardize Trump's political resurrection.

We can assume that the Trumpists will split into at least two groups: those who will resign themselves to accepting Joe Biden's victory and those who will continue to believe the election was stolen. The latter will seek to share their "fascist[38]" belief with as many Americans as possible. Given the importance of evangelical "Christian nationalism" in pro-Trump movements, the second possibility seems more likely, unless the "believers" are isolated[39].

Belonging to a group or not seems to be a determining variable in continuing to believe. Isolated people tend to abandon their dissonant belief because they feel powerless over the shock of disillusionment. Conversely, belonging to a group makes the suffering easier to bear. Modern digital social networks allow the formation and continued existence of groups beyond disillusionment.

Proselytizing, i.e. the collective dissemination of an individual invention, is at the heart of innovation processes, whether the innovation is perceived as negative or positive. Innovation is subject to a principle of symmetry. It is neither easier nor more difficult for a "good" or a "bad" innovation to spread. In the consumer sector, the diffusion of organic products and electric cars is still very marginal today, but both seem to have moved beyond the "militancy" stage. As for political models, the populist versions with a conspiracy foundation are the ones that are spreading[40].

Conspiracy theories are the political aspect of what we call rumours and urban legends. Paranoia, conspiracy theories and witchcraft show the permanence of conspiracy phenomena, under various names, throughout history and societies. This persecutory aspect of the imaginary is also part of the process by which innovations spread, because innovators may feel rejected by the competitors or groups receiving the new invention[41].

This process of moving from invention to innovation may take several years before the innovation becomes widespread beyond the pioneer group.

Christian Jewish Proselytism Remains a Transgressive Practice in Judea, Galilee and Among the Diaspora

The mechanisms for resolving cognitive dissonance would appear to be anthropological invariants. The imaginaries mobilized to resolve the dissonance obviously vary according to culture and era. They seem to have been used to manage many "post-crisis recoveries", including after the destruction of the Temple in Jerusalem.

In order to survive, the rabbinic Judaism current focussed on Jewish tradition and gradually abandoned proselytism, especially after the fifth century and the political success of Christianity in the Roman Empire. The Hellenistic Christian Jews chose another survival strategy: converting the pagans by relaxing the rules of Judaism. The dominant Greco-Roman polytheism was faced with two minority monotheistic competitors.

The proselytism of the early Christian Jews appears to be a survival strategy for Judaism and one of the possible solutions to their messianic cognitive dissonance. However, for a Jew in the first century AD, being a convert still constituted a breach of Judean tradition, even though it had been happening for two centuries and Judaism was gaining some traction among the Middle Eastern and Mediterranean elites.

There was a "horizon of expectation"[42], a mental framework that supported receiving the message. To certain Greco-Roman pagans, monotheism seemed to belong to the social elite, as if it were superior to polytheism. This horizon of expectation would be widely used by the future Christianity. However, to succeed, some of the cultural barriers that hindered the spread of the monotheistic belief in the Greco-Roman environment had to be lowered, while incorporating some of the pagan practices of the host environment.

Conversions to Judaism seem to have continued for a few centuries more. In around 135—which is when the Jews of Judea lost their last major war with the Romans, a revolt led by Simon Bar Kokhba, who was himself very much opposed to the Christian Jews—the emperor Hadrian forbade the Jews from converting the rest of the population to their religion. He "prohibited all circumcision"[43]. According to Shlomo Sand, the fact that some Hellenistic males perceived circumcision as a threat to their identity explains why a share of these newly converted Jews were women, because they "did not have to undergo circumcision, a severe commandment that aroused great reluctance among the converts"[44]. This ban on circumcision is a further indication that some Jewish clerics were indeed proselytizing.

There were probably Jewish kingdoms of non-Judean origin in Yemen and Ethiopia around the fourth and sixth centuries, although there is no consensus as to their existence. Forms of Persian, Jewish and Christian monotheism reached the countries of southern Arabia[45]. Although it remains to be verified, this may also be true of Ethiopia and the Kingdom of Aksum in the north (in modern Tigray), where some Christian traditions today appear to be similar to Hebrew rituals, as in Lalibela. The Ethiopian Jews who emigrated to Israel from 1977 onwards came from Tigray.

The issue of proselytizing is an indicator of the possible tensions between Jewish and Roman practices as well as the paradoxical position of the Christian-Jewish innovation. In the Judean world it was perceived as a transgression of the rules of purity and in the Roman world as a superstition (*superstitio*) and hence a threat.

Paradoxically, despite the obstacles of circumcision and kashrut, Judaism spread relatively well, as far as Mesopotamia and beyond. Like any innovation, Judaism was ambivalent. While it clashed with the dominant polytheistic norm, which was quite flexible when it came to deities, it attracted people seeking to differentiate themselves from conventional religions.

In turn, the religion that would later become Christianity expanded geographically via these same Jewish settlements, because it offered them a "simplified Judaism", at least when it came to rituals. What mainly put an end to Jewish proselytism was the political victory of Christianity from the fourth century onwards, under the emperor Constantine. In order to continue to spread, the Christian Jewish innovation sought to distance itself from its Jewish origins and adapt to Greco-Roman culture.

*

The debate over making accommodations on circumcision and kashrut, which was part of the larger power struggles between the different factions of first-century Judaism—the Judeo-Christians with James, the Hellenistic Christian Jews with Paul, the Pharisees, Essenes, Zealots and Sadducees—did not end there. It was regularly debated in most of the synagogues around the Mediterranean for one or two centuries and probably longer. Eventually, in the late first century, it would cause the Christian Jews to be expelled from the synagogues, which led them to develop their monotheistic invention independently, though not without clashes with the dominant polytheism.

At the start of the first century, thanks to Paul, the Christian Jewish movement simplified purification rituals, which included immersion in water, a ritual that originated with the Essenes, and abolished circumcision and kashrut. This simplification established significant discontinuity with traditional Judaism. At the same time, he kept but reinterpreted three key elements of the Torah: monotheism, the ability for non-Jews to convert, and, above all, the belief in eternal life and thus in the existence of a better world after death. These three elements of continuity would play a role in the religious innovation's reception, because they aligned with the horizon of expectation of those among the Greco-Roman elite who were open to monotheism.

Belief in resurrection served to enchant the ignominious catastrophe of Jesus' death on a cross. Enchanting the invention releases the imaginary from the cognitive dissonance experienced when the Messiah does not return[46]. The human network disseminating the religious invention (the Jewish diaspora), the places where this occurred (the synagogues), the simplification of practices and rituals and the enchantment of Jesus' death became the logistical, social and symbolic pillars of the development of the Hellenistic Christian Jewish innovation, especially after the destruction of the Temple.

~ ~ ~

Chapter 7

The Destruction of the Temple: The Incremental Invention Becomes a Disruptive Innovation

Between 66 and 70 AD, Palestine was at a turning point. It was a time of great messianic hope and also concerns about Israel's security and survival. The Zealots' politico-religious protest movement was growing in Galilee, in northern Palestine. The Pharisees were not particularly for it, fearing a repressive Roman response that would include sacking the Temple, just as the victorious Babylonians had done in the second century BC when they then deported the Jewish elite to Babylon. However, they found themselves much like Cassandra in Greek mythology, "the useless prophet" given the gift of predicting the future and at the same time the curse of never being believed[1].

Unlike in the religions of Antiquity whose gods were human creations, for the Jews, their sacred texts speak or comment on the word of God[2]. They were written down at the same time as the Torah and then the Gospels, between 700 BC and 400 AD[3]. Following Norman Golb's interpretation, this climate of anxiety explains why some of the Temple books were moved to safety before the year 70, to Qumran, a strategic location for monitoring the Dead Sea, which was a key zone for civilian and military transit[4].

70 AD: Jesus' Invention Seems on the Verge of Disappearing

At the beginning of the Zealot's revolt, the group of Judeo-Christians around James the Just and the group of Hellenistic Christian Jews who followed Peter and Paul, not to mention the uncircumcised Gentiles converted by Paul, seemed on the verge of disappearing. They represented barely a few thousand people out of the Roman Empire's population of 70 million, a number based on a fragile hypothesis and which Enrico Norelli cites with caution[5], but it still gives us an order of magnitude.

Paul was tried for subversion in around 67 and sentenced to death by beheading and not by hanging, because he was a Roman citizen. He was executed in Rome. James the Just was condemned by a Sadducean high priest and stoned to death outside Jerusalem's walls in around 60. Peter was also eliminated The question of whether or not he was executed in Rome is a point on which Catholics and Protestants disagree. If Saint Peter did not die in Rome, it calls into question the historical pre-eminence of the Pope of Rome on which the central power of the Catholic religion is based.

The innovation's three main mobilizing figures are now gone, the Messiah has not returned and the Temple appears to be threatened because of the Zealots' revolt and potential Roman repression ahead. Everything is unstable. There is great anxiety in Galilee and Judea. The monotheistic invention reinterpreted by Jesus seems to have run its course.

The Christian Jewish currents could have dissolved within the various factions of Judaism and never ultimately have emerged as a new religion. Nobody would have bet one denarius—the currency of the time—on the future of these different currents. The 'invention of Christianity' could have ended there and never become an innovation that would mark the whole of western Eurasia for countless centuries, right up to the present day. And yet, these different currents of Judaism, including what would be Christianity, were likely given their chance by the unexpected arrival of a "black swan[6]".

The Constant Ambivalence of Crises: Between Risk and Opportunity

Throughout human history, crises have always been both risks and opportunities. In Chinese, the word *crisis* is *Wēijī* (危机), which is composed from *Wēixiǎn* (危险, danger) and *Jīhuì* (机会, opportunity). This is why the metaphor of the black swan, already mentioned above, is useful for understanding innovation processes. It explains most failures to predict the success or failure of an invention, and more generally of a major change. The black swan, the crisis, the unforeseen event, such as the destruction of the Temple in 70 AD, the 2008 financial crisis, COVID-19 in 2020, or the war in Ukraine in 2022, collides with the "mental tunnels[7]" that organize decision-makers' calculations and futurists' projections, irrespective of the level of decision-making, be it central or local.

These cognitive tunnels are based on the trust decision-makers place in long series or cycles, believing they will continue unchanged for a long time. The series becomes a collective norm. There are no societies without norms and social constraints. The history of societies can be summed up as the passage from one dominant norm to another, as expressed in the myth of Sisyphus revisited by Camus[8]. The norm allows for routine and life in society, but it limits the perception of future crises.

The common norm conditions life in society because it allows integration into a social group, as the social psychologist Muzafer Sherif showed in 1935 with the "autokinetic effect". In this experiment, people were taken one by one into a completely dark room and shown a dot of light. The dot was immobile but had the appearance of moving ("autokinetic effect"). When asked individually how far the dot moved, people make different estimates. However, once they are brought together as a group, they will gradually arrive at a common norm. The emergence of this norm explains the shift from invention to innovation, from production to reception, i.e. here, the passage from Jewish monotheism to Christian monotheism, then its reception and reinterpretation by polytheism.

However, no established social order can be explained just by showing that there are no societies without group norms and thus without social control. All this shows is that there are no societies without power relations and that innovation processes are crisscrossed with these power relations. This is why crises that are destructive also offer windows of opportunity because they disrupt situations that are blocked by cognitive tunnels. Actors and their survival are most at risk when they believe they are eternal.

Could the Romans have imagined that monotheism would one day become the Empire's dominant religion? Could the Saducean priests and later the rabbis fighting for the survival of Judaism and the Jewish people have imagined that a tiny start-up with a few hundred members launched by Jesus would threaten their positions? This is unlikely.

It is an illusion to believe that if we connect all the events seemingly related to the innovation's success, then the innovation process has been reconstructed. This fails to take into account all the wrong turns, failed inventions, unforeseen events and the interplay of actors that make it uncertain that the invention will turn into an innovation—in other words, that the message of Jesus will turn into a religion, Christianity, some hundred years after his death. The inventors of Christianity themselves made extensive use of this retrospective illusion by using all the texts liable to prove that Jesus was indeed the awaited Messiah.

Another illusion involves looking for texts by individuals who had foreseen the catastrophe, and of course such texts can always be found, especially in apocalyptic literature from the past or present. These people, it will be said, had been right in their predictions but nobody wanted to see it and hence there was a "conspiracy" of silence, a "denial of reality", which was being "hidden" from us. This is to forget that most "prophets of doom" spend twenty, thirty or fifty years predicting disasters and that crises happen from time to time to make us believe the predictions were reliable. One need only read the prophets who announced Israel's destruction or punishment in the Old Testament.

Without the destruction of the Temple in Jerusalem in 70 AD, the unexpected "black swan" event, the invention of Christian Jewish monotheism might not have continued to spread. This spread became possible thanks to spatial dispersion and the decentralization of Jewish religious authority to the synagogues in Galilee and around the Mediterranean rim, and in Asia Minor and the Tigris and Euphrates region. The synagogues had been established outside Jerusalem "among those Judeans who could not visit the Temple regularly". Thanks to the synagogues, "Judaism overcame the crisis triggered by the destruction of the single sanctuary and managed to survive as a people"[9].

They were also an opportunity for the Jewish current that followed Jesus. The end of the Temple "triggered the decline and even the disappearance of the Sadducees, Essenes and Zealots and favoured the rise of the Pharisees and Rabbis"[10]. The Judeo-Christians who followed James the Just would also disappear. Until the destruction of the Temple, Christian Jews and circumcised Gentile converts, regardless of their tendency, were factions within the different currents of Judaism.

The Destruction of the Temple: A Window of Opportunity for the Emergence of Rabbinic Judaism

After their revolt in Galilee, the Zealots moved south into Judea and occupied Jerusalem. This revolt was met with a violent backlash from the Roman army, which resulted in the destruction of the Temple in 70 AD by Titus, the son of the emperor Vespasian. With the end of the Temple, the central political and religious power of the priests disappeared. This disappearance can be seen as the event that triggered the transition from the incremental invention of purifying Judaism (the aim of the Pharisees, the Essenes, Jesus and then his brother James the Just) to disruptive innovation, namely opening Judaism to the Gentiles so as to strengthen Judaism in the western and eastern Mediterranean (the aim of several Jewish factions, including Paul's). Paul himself had already laid the groundwork for this shift from the incremental to the disruptive.

Paul's story shows that a disruptive innovation cannot be decreed. It is the result of a historical process that is itself the fruit of an aggregation of numerous decisions that lead to incremental changes, in small, nonlinear steps, because this development process can be punctuated by crises.

Christianity is the result of two Jewish survival strategies, one focussed on its "core business", rabbinic Judaism, and the other embarking on a race to expand through proselytizing and simplifying daily rituals for the new "target", the "pagans" from the ancient religions. After the destruction of the Temple, everything in the religion had to be entirely rebuilt. Simon Claude Mimouni writes that "there is a certain filiation between the Pharisees and the rabbis, and the latter are the successors, at least spiritually, of the former[11]". To simplify, the Pharisee movement, which was highly developed in Galilee during the reign of Herod and at the time of Jesus, had two founding fathers, Hillel and Shammai. The House of Shammai (Beit Shammai) is believed to have been the more stringent of the two. Any historical reconstruction of the lives of these Pharisee sages is no more certain than that of Jesus. The sources are uncertain to say the least and often border on the fantastical, such as the story of how Rabban Yohanan ben Zakkai, one of the founders of rabbinic Judaism, escaped the siege of Jerusalem inside a coffin[12].

With the destruction of the Temple, Judaism became an endangered religion at risk of extinction, and the Jews as a people along with it. Everything had to be reinvented, which created an enormous opportunity for innovation. Rabbinic Judaism and Christianity took advantage of the opportunity presented by the Temple's disappearance to recast themselves. Unexpectedly, the recasting of Judaism would lead to the emergence of a new religion in the second century AD, even though this was not the aim of the inventor Jesus nor of his disciples. Christianity appears to be the Hellenistic reinterpretation of the Jewish-Christian recasting of rabbinic Judaism.

After the destruction of the Temple, the rabbi Yohanan ben Zakkai set about reviving Judaism by founding a school (*yeshiva*) in Yavne. He belonged to the House of Hillel, which was less rigid than that of Shammai, making him more consensual, which is a considerable asset when it comes to federating energies. He is considered to be the "founder of the rabbinic academies that emerged after 70"[13]. They were to serve as the historical foundation for rabbinic Judaism. This current was opposed to the Temple priests, like Jesus in his time[14].

> In the aftermath of the Temple's destruction, Yohanan ben Zakkai appears to have transformed his academy into an "assembly" or "synod", with the aim of replacing the lost Sanhedrin [...] he issued nine edicts which were deemed indispensable for Judean worship, since they included the dates of fast days, feast days and the beginning of the months. Previously, such tasks were performed by the high priest and the Sanhedrin[15].

The sanctuary having disappeared and the Sadducean priests having lost their power, Yohanan ben Zakkai set about rebuilding Judaism, with the Romans' agreement. He declared that God no longer demanded sacrifice, a very important practical change to the rituals, but also for the religion's logistics.

Some Jewish currents had long been opposed to the Temple's sacrificial practices, which they felt had too much in common with Greco-Roman ones. The ritual required animals to be killed and burned so that the smell would please God[16]. It was an important purification ritual for anyone who had been rendered impure by failing to follow certain religious rules. This is probably part of the reason why Rabbi Ben Zakkai and Jesus objected to the sacrifices in the Temple. This shows that in the first century, prayer became more important than material sacrifice.

In terms of organization, performing these sacrificial rituals required a space as large as the Temple with enough room for the merchants, the money changers and the animals awaiting sacrifice. From a logistical standpoint, eliminating sacrificial practices was a way of adapting to the new situation after losing this central space in Jerusalem, the Temple. Without the organizational burden of sacrifices, the synagogues, which were much smaller spaces, could now take over. Eliminating ritual sacrifices was a revolutionary innovation, adopted under exceptional situational constraints and that gave Judaism greater autonomy in terms of space and organization. It gave it the flexibility to adapt to the diversity of the Jewish diaspora scattered around the Mediterranean. Sacrifices were replaced by prayer, the reading of texts and by the written rules of the Mishna.

Yohanan ben Zakkai's (?–80/85) successor as "the head of the Yavne academy" was Rabbi Gamaliel II (?–138/140)[17]. He was the son of Gamaliel I, who was Paul the Apostle's teacher. For Etienne Nodet, Gamaliel II was "the true founder of rabbinic Judaism[18]". All of this demonstrates that the different actors were part of the same Jewish Pharisaic culture, in the broad sense, which was divided into different currents, each following a pre-eminent rabbi, be it Yohanan ben Zakkai, Gamaliel or Jesus. Gamaliel II continued to set the dates in Judaism's ritual calendar. He also "appointed judges and pronounced anathemas against those Judeans judged to be deviant or apostate [...] It was he [...] who tackled the Christian Judeans, notably by anathematizing Rabbi Eliezer ben Hurcanus for allegedly sympathizing with the message of Jesus of Nazareth[19]". The Gospel of Matthew, which is critical of the Pharisees, takes particular aim at the Yavne movement[20].

Another rabbi who played an important role in the renewal of Judaism was Rabbi Akiva ben Joseph (50–132/135). There was much apologetic competition in Judaism, and he helped to fix the canonical texts of the Torah in Hebrew just as the Hellenistic Christian Jews who were also fixing theirs in Greek.

Disagreements Over the Interpretation of the Torah, or the Competition Between the Gospels and the Mishna

The story of the origins of rabbinic Judaism, however uncertain, gives us a better understanding of the strategic and historical role of the Gospels. The different Jewish communities were divided by various debates, of which the Gospels were a part. Each community offered its own interpretation of the Torah and of the applicable rules. These texts were also tools that provided arguments and justifications in the competition between rabbinic and Christian Jewish currents.

Initially then, the Gospels were part of the debate that contributed to Judaism's rebirth throughout the first century AD in Judea, Galilee and among the Jewish diaspora in both the East and the West, probably until the first half of the second century.

The objective of the Christian Jews was to convince the other current that Jesus was indeed the expected Messiah and that by his resurrection, he had fulfilled the Scriptures by reinterpreting them with new meaning. They also sought to present arguments to the polytheistic world in which they sought to expand. The writing in the Gospels reflects this need to be received into both the Jewish and polytheistic worlds. The Gospel according to Mark seems to be aimed at a Roman audience, while Matthew is aimed at the emerging current of rabbinic Judaism.

The four Gospels were written in different geographical and cultural locations in the Mediterranean region. They were therefore partly influenced by the ongoing debates within the communities that followed Jesus. Christian tradition typically identifies the Gospels of Mark, Matthew and Luke as synoptic Gospels, as they contain comparable accounts of Jesus' life. They are distinct from the Gospel of John, which is crafted in a literary and theological style comparable to that of Revelation[21]. John's Book of Revelation contains a rendering of the prevailing political concerns in Judea. All of them, with the possible exception of Mark, were written after the destruction of the Temple in Jerusalem.

The Gospel of Mark was probably written in Rome[22] either shortly before or after the 70s. Matthew and Luke were written between the 80s and 90s. They tell the story of Jesus' life and present him as a prophet or messiah who will save the people of Israel. Luke and the Acts of the Apostles appear to reflect the Pauline tradition. Daniel Marguerat, who comes from the Protestant tradition, offers a subtle narrative analysis of the Acts of the Apostles that takes the codes in Luke and renders them in the context of the time[23]. The synoptic Gospels are crucial for understanding the historical spread of Christian monotheism in the late first and early second centuries.

Disagreements over the Interpretation of the Torah 95

The Gospel of John was written in Asia Minor[24] much later on, around the year 100, and is a more allegorical text than the synoptic Gospels. According to Enrico Norelli, John's text tells the story that preceded Jesus, that of "Israel's infidelity [according to John] and inability to understand its own Scriptures (John 5:45–47); [the rest of the text recounts] the difficult life of the community that must [testify about] Jesus in a hostile Jewish 'world' that rejects the message of Jesus and rejects those Jews who believe in him (John 9:22)"[25]. The text is a good indication of this Christian Jewish current's sense of belonging to Judaism.

The Gospel of John (9:22) laments that "the Jews had agreed already that if anyone confessed that He was Christ, he would be put out of the synagogue". We are at the heart of the debate with rabbinic Judaism, if we read the Gospel as both an account of Jesus' life and an expression of the situation of Christian Jews fifty to seventy years later, in their battle with the orthodoxy of rabbinic Judaism where each actor is fighting for the survival of Israel.

From a historical point of view, it is very difficult to distinguish between the words Jesus spoke during his lifetime and those attributed to him forty or seventy years after his death. For example, some exegetes believe that the text of the Beatitudes was probably spoken by Jesus himself. The reliability of the spoken versus the written word is not the source of uncertainty. Transmission in societies with an oral tradition is more or less as reliable as with monastic scribes. I found this to be true in my genealogical studies of kinship in the Congo[26]. But both the oral and the written word can be manipulated over time according to prevailing social issues. In the Congo, certain people would be eliminated from the oral family genealogy following a conflict with the head of the family. We need only remember how the Scriptures mistreated Cain and the Kenites to understand how social memory is selective and how it can organize the facts according to the issues of the time.

Matthew wrote his Gospel in Syria-Palestine[27], ten to twenty years after the destruction of the Temple. He echoes the debates with the Pharisee rabbis who emerged around Yavne (or Yavneh), west of Jerusalem, and later in Galilee: "And so it was, when Jesus had ended these sayings, that the people were astonished at His teaching, for He taught them as one having authority, and not as the scribes" (Matt. 7:28–29). Jesus spoke like a rabbi.

However, his words can be attributed as much to Jesus challenging the priestly caste of the Sadducees in his lifetime as they can be to the debates between Pharisees and Christian Jews forty years later. Matthew contains numerous reports of debates between Jesus and the Pharisees on the issue of ritual practices. Some of these debates probably took place in Jesus' time and others when the Gospels were written, meaning the debates were with Judaism's sages as the Mishna was being fixed in writing[28]. At the same time, Greco-Roman mythology was also fixed in writing, although the Bibliotheca of Pseudo-Apollodorus indicates that this occurred a little later, in the second century AD[29]. Oral tradition was no longer enough to compete on the market of ideas. It now had to be fixed in writing all around the Mediterranean.

As Enrico Norelli writes: "Matthew targets [...] the rabbis as they sought to rebuild Judaism after the catastrophe of 70—the destruction of the Temple—and close ranks around Torah law according to the Pharisee tradition, by also tracing the oral tradition back to the revelation in the Sinai and using this to build what would be called a 'fence for the Torah', i.e. a system of rules designed to ensure its observance[30]". For the rabbis, guaranteeing observance of the Law was equivalent to guaranteeing the survival of Judaism.

One of the debates within the first-century Jewish communities was over whether or not to interpret the Law and the Prophets, as Jesus and as Rabbi ben Zakkai did, even though certain historians say that some of their coreligionists felt they were not the most legitimate. One hypothesis is that the Gospels are indeed part of this debate and that this was the central debate in Judaism between 70 and perhaps the middle of the second century AD.

*

This hypothesis becomes plausible if, as I do as an anthropologist, we analyze the emergence of Christian Judaism in terms of the situation (the first-century Jewish people were in a situation in which their survival was threatened) and the power relations between the various legitimate actors engaged in the social game, and all of this under the constraint of survival. Thus we are not analyzing the theological content of the Mishnah and the Gospels but the practices put in place to ensure the survival of the new "post-Temple" Judaism.

One of the ways of legitimizing the Christian Jews' strategic practice was to not only use texts from the Hebrew Bible to show that Jesus was indeed the one the prophets foretold, but also to write down his oral commentaries on the Torah. These commentaries were fixed in Aramaic and Syriac, a "dialect of Aramaic, a language itself derived from Hebrew[31]". Writing the Gospels in Greek was a way to reach a broader receiving audience, but at the risk of betraying Jesus. Putting his words on paper was a strategy to equip the Christian Jews with a stronger set of arguments to compete with the rabbinic current. The Gospel of Matthew provides a clear understanding of the troubled links between rabbinic and Christian Judaism, for those Jews who believed that Jesus was the Messiah, *Massiah* in Hebrew and *Christos* in Greek. It sheds light on how the synagogues would act as the relays in this battle between factions of Judaism throughout the Mediterranean. The invention was being transformed into innovation and reinterpreted by its Greco-Roman world of reception.

~ ~ ~

Chapter 8

The Struggle Between Rabbinic Judaism and Christianity for Control of the Synagogues

Because both monotheisms fixed the rules of the Oral Torah in writing, they were subsequently used to expel Christian Jews from the synagogues and for the Christians to reject rabbinic Judaism as a false belief. The two main currents on the market of religious ideas were themselves internally very diverse and addressed the same population, the same "cognitive market" to use Gérald Bronner's expression[1], namely the Jews of the Diaspora and the populations attracted by Judaism and gravitating towards synagogues or places of prayer. The battle was over whether those who wished to convert should be subject to the strict rules of Judaism or to more-relaxed ones.

As a group, the Hellenistic Christian Jews, who recognized Jesus as the Messiah announced in the Scriptures, were engaged in a dual process of exclusion and integration that they had not expressly chosen. The first was a process of separation from the group of Judean Jews, which saw their proselytism as lenient, because it was based on less-rigorous rules, or as we would say today on less-professional criteria that lower the quality of the service. The second was a quest for integration into the Greco-Roman world which, on the contrary, sought to assemble multiple deities with no need for the exclusivity offered by monotheism. Ensuring the reception of Christian Jewish monotheism by polytheism proved as problematic as its diffusion within rabbinic Judaism.

For those who felt torn between the Jewish and Greco-Roman poles, especially if they were of Jewish origin, all this was a tragedy and a source of suffering[2]. Innovation does not only disrupt technology or services, it also disrupts social relations among human groups. This disruption is often the sign that an innovation is progressing.

How the Use of Greek Nourished the Emerging Theology of Christianity

Both groups still shared the same book, the Torah. As Simon Claude Mimouni writes: "After the destruction of the Temple of Jerusalem and the disappearance of its institutions, the Judeans, of all persuasions, had only one common asset left: the Torah[3]". The battle was over the interpretation of the sacred texts. This interpretation began to diverge more and more throughout the second and third centuries, not only for theological reasons, but also for linguistic ones.

Mary, the mother of Jesus, is the best-known example of variation in meaning linked to the shift from Hebrew to Greek. In the Hebrew Bible, in the book of the prophet Isaiah (7:14), it is written "Look, the *young woman* is with child and about to give birth to a son. Let her name him Immanuel"[4]. This ancient text, which was in Hebrew, makes no mention of a virgin. Yet it is this same text from Isaiah that is reused in the Gospel of Matthew to announce the virgin birth of Jesus: "Behold, a *virgin* shall conceive and bear a son, and his name shall be called Emmanuel" (Matt. 1:23; drawn from Isa. 7:14; emphasis by the author). With the help of my old dictionary of ancient Greek, I looked up the original version of the text in Matthew, which was written in Greek and uses the word *parthenos* (παρθένος), which means virgin. Didier Long confirms that even Paul, "when he speaks of Mary, uses the Greek term *gunè* (γυνή) ('woman') and not *parthenos* ('virgin')[5]".

There was what is known as a "semantic shift", a shift in meaning. It has led to heated theological debates about Mary's virginity, particularly between Catholics and Protestants, with Protestant Christians contesting this virginity. In passing from Hebrew to Greek, the status of the mother of Jesus changed. She went from being a young woman to a virgin, which over the centuries produced complex theology on the negative relationship to the body or to matter in relation to original sin.

Justin was an important second-century Christian author because he provides an indication of the ongoing separation between Jews and Christians. He wrote of the existence of "virgin mothers" in Greco-Roman mythology[6]. The best-known example is Athena, the virgin mother of the first Athenian in Greek mythology[7].

However, Greek thought was not only transmitted by language. It was also a philosophical encounter, especially the Neoplatonism of the third century with Plotinus (205–270), who spoke in Greek. The philosopher Michel Piclin reminds us in his guide to Plotinus that "the Greek language contains a whole range of concepts where it is difficult to specify whether they are Platonic or Hebraic, or even Oriental[8]". Given its diversity, the Greek language appears to have been a melting pot for Eastern and Western thought. There is a kind of homology between the forges of the Kenites and the Greek language.

This enduring belief in the Virgin Mary, which emerged between the second and third centuries, eventually produced the nineteenth-century dogma of the Immaculate Conception (1854), which affirms that the Virgin Mary was born without original sin. As early as the first and second centuries, reference is made to the virgin birth of Jesus to a woman, the Virgin Mary, who did not "know" a man. The belief in the Assumption of the mother of Jesus, i.e. her ascent into heaven in an uncorrupted body, first appeared around the seventh century in Eastern Christianity.

Another term that has also given rise to debate, as I have already mentioned, is "brother of Jesus", applied to James the Just: *adelphos* (αδελφός) in Greek. This can be used in the sense of biological brother or "classificatory brother", a common concept in the anthropology of kinship that groups brothers and cousins into one category or class.

These two examples are indicators of the progressive separation of the Hebrew Jewish current of the rabbis, who came from the group of Pharisees that emerged after the destruction of the Temple, from the Hellenistic Christian Jewish current that followed Jesus, which was in the process of separating from Judaism and would become the Christian current in the first century AD. They are also indicators of the intense intermixing of Eastern and Western philosophical and religious thought.

At this time of intellectual effervescence in the Mediterranean world, which stretched as far as the Iranian plains bordering the steppes of Central Asia, all beliefs were intertwined and influenced each other. Michel Piclin writes that it is not surprising that Plotinus' work appealed to the Christians. In his *Enneads*, he speaks of "the *logos* by which the universal soul governs the cosmos[9]". This text echoes the opening of the Gospel according to John, written one hundred and fifty years earlier: "In the beginning was the Word [*logos*, λόγος], and the Word was with God, and the Word was God [...] All things were made by him; and without him was not anything made that was made. In him was life; and the life was the light of men" (John 1:1–4).

In the religious practices of Hellenistic Christian Jews, especially in Alexandria in Egypt[10], the use of Greek would become predominant through the reading of both the Septuagint and the New Testament, which was also in Greek. It is possible that the Gospels of Matthew and Luke, of which only the Greek version is known, were written from a common text in Aramaic, which was the language of Jesus. There is no longer any trace of this text, which is known as the "Q source".

Over two or three centuries, all of this led to a wider and wider separation between the Hellenistic Jewish groups and the Hebrew and Aramaic speakers. By now it is clear that the unity of Judaism could not be maintained with the use of a dual language system. Language does not explain the separation, but it does account for the social and linguistic conditions of that separation.

The invention of monotheism gradually became an innovation that spread throughout the Greco-Roman world in the form of a reinterpretation of the Hebrew Bible (including the Torah) that became the Christian Bible, with an Old Testament and a New Testament. Christianity began as messianism before becoming a belief in the divinity of Jesus. As Frédéric Lenoir summarizes, "at the dawn of the second century, people were still beating about the bush over the divinity of Jesus [...] the debate about the identity of Jesus [...] had only just begun[11]". It was not until somewhere between the mid-second and mid-third century that the Apostles' Creed appeared. This "was the result of the fusion that occurred in Rome between 150 and 250 between a Christological formula, i.e. that Jesus is indeed the Messiah, and a Trinitarian formula, [i.e.] that Jesus is the Son of God[12]":

> I believe in God, the Father almighty, creator of heaven and earth. I believe in Jesus Christ, God's only Son, our Lord, who was conceived by the Holy Spirit, born of the Virgin Mary, suffered under Pontius Pilate, was crucified, died, and was buried; he descended to the dead. On the third day he rose again; he ascended into heaven, he is seated at the right hand of the Father, and he will come to judge the living and the dead. I believe in the Holy Spirit, the holy catholic Church, the communion of saints, the forgiveness of sins, the resurrection of the body, and the life everlasting.

This text marks the complete break between the tradition of rabbinic Judaism and emerging Christianity.

Apologetic Competition Between the Mishna and the Gospels

To shed light on the development strategies within the two emerging strands of Judaism, we must go back in time a little. After the exile in the sixth century BC, Babylon continued to be an important centre for Judaism and even gave its name to one of the two great sacred books, the "Babylonian Talmud". Later, around the sixth century AD, this would become the most important text in Judaism. It includes the Mishna, which fixed the oral commentaries of the Torah in writing[13]. Norman Golb explains that the Mishnah was written down from the first century AD onwards by descendants of the Pharisees, the *Tannaim*. They were the very first rabbis, who at the time were not priests but lay sages.

Both the chronology and the filiation are disputed and must be taken with caution. They are helpful mostly in focussing our attention on the relative importance of these sacred books compared to the poems of Greco-Roman mythology. The latter express and transform that mythology, whose diversity is a response to day-to-day situations. They highlight the difference in conception between monotheistic sacred books, which set out rules and beliefs, and polytheistic and philosophical texts, one of whose functions is to seek to render everyday actions more efficient, whether via the influence of the "Lares", the household gods, or of the deities who served as guarantors of good harvests or health. What both these approaches to religion have in common is that they convey meaning and collective identity. And if there is one human aspect on which human beings struggle to negotiate among themselves, it is meaning and identity.

The Mishna, the oral law, determines what work is forbidden on the Sabbath, such as the preparation of food[14]. Judaism's sacred books fix the rules for ritual purification and the calendar of religious holidays. These rules were all the more important because they were a central issue in the power struggles between the orthodox rabbinic majority and the heterodox Hellenistic Christian Jewish minority. Setting the rules helped influence the course of the social process by which the monotheistic innovation spread within or beyond Judaism.

The important point for understanding the innovation process is that these commentaries, which began to be set down after the destruction of the Temple[15], were fixed at the same time as the Gospels and part of the

New Testament were written. The oral commentaries on the Torah were compiled and arranged in around the third century, in parallel with the fixation of the Christian canon by Irenaeus (c. 130–c. 202), Bishop of Lyon and one of the "Church Fathers", in reference to the founders of Christianity. This parallelism is indicative of "apologetic competition", a race to defend the truth between the different currents of Judaism from the first to the fourth century AD.

Paul the Apostle already described this competition in the First Epistle to the Corinthians: "Now I say this, that each of you says, 'I am of Paul', or 'I am of Apollos', or 'I am of Cephas', or 'I am of Christ'" (1 Cor. 1:12). In the Epistle to the Galatians, he also affirmed his Jewishness: "We who are Jews by nature, and not sinners of the [uncircumcised] Gentiles" (Gal. 2:15). The birth of Christianity was a painful and contentious process.

This confirms that we are witnessing competition between currents that both identify with Judaism, and one of which follows a *rabbi* or master who is close to the Pharisees on the issue of resurrection. He goes by the name of Jesus and little by little would be named Christ, Messiah, and more specifically the Crucified and Risen Christ. By fixing the canonical rules in writing, each side could differentiate those that were true from those that were false, from their own point of view.

The Battle of the Synagogues a Matter of Survival for the Jewish People

Despite the destruction of "its unique sanctuary", Judaism's different factions survived thanks to the synagogues but at the cost of a fracture within Judaism, from which the Christian movement would emerge[16]. This movement was no more unified than Judaism until the Council of Nicaea in Anatolia in 325.

The spread of Jewish Christianity followed the network of synagogues where the Jewish diaspora worshipped[17]. Etienne Nodet believes that the oldest synagogues emerged in the third century BC, around 250 BC, in Egypt. Synagogues were "places of study and of prayer[18]". According to Simon Claude Mimouni and Pierre Maraval, "in Rome, in the first century, there were about fifteen synagogues". Whatever their form, the Jews had places to meet and pray, which were called synagogues, as mentioned in the Acts of the Apostles (17:1).

As historian Paul Geoltrain writes: "The communities of the 'Jesus movement' [...] were close to the synagogues of the Diaspora (one need only lay a map of the Christian settlements over one of the synagogues existing at the time to see that they overlap almost entirely)[19]". This "pre-digital" human network had been around for some time. It was formed several centuries before in Alexandria and Babylon as a result of deportations, but also of voluntary migration, often linked to trade, and conversions, even if the term probably had a different, perhaps more collective, connotation than today. Here it refers to the practice of changing religious affiliation by adopting new rituals, whether by personal conviction, because of a shift in the norm of the group and particularly of the chief, king or head of the family, or by physical coercion.

The Jewish world developed within the Roman Empire, but not exclusively. There were Jewish communities in eastern Mesopotamia, which was not part of the Empire. The Empire facilitated the circulation of people, goods and information. "The Empire was bilingual: Latin was used for legal and administrative texts, but Greek remained the language of all kinds of exchanges (commercial and intellectual). Thus, anyone educated had to be able to read and write Latin and Greek[20]". *Koinè*, the common Greek language, was therefore the language of communication, even if the Aramaic language and culture prevailed in the eastern Empire[21]. For Simon Claude Mimouni and Pierre Maraval, the size of the Mediterranean Jewish diaspora, which extended as far as the Parthian Empire in the first century, helps us "to understand how Christianity spread so easily throughout the entire Mediterranean basin[22]".

Indeed, most inventions do not spread in a social vacuum. They follow lines of force, namely the social networks that organize any society, rather like the contour lines on a map indicate how steep a slope is and thus how fast the rivers flow.

I did my first study on "pre-digital" social networks between 1969 and 1971 (with the participation of Jean-Pierre Worms, under the direction of Michel Crozier and Erhard Friedberg), looking at the French *Corps des Mines*. This helped me understand that there were no societies without social networks and that these were the collective vectors that spread change, decision-making processes and innovations[23]. There is no society without social networks, and no innovation spreads without a pre-existing social network. In the case of Christianity, it was the Jewish diaspora that played this role.

It is interesting to note that this theological competition is not unique to the religious world. It can be transposed to the modern world of new digital technologies. Today, technical and scientific arguments have replaced the religious arguments of the past. And today, as in the past, there is a gap between what the engineers, or theologians, say about the technical quality of a digital application and the end-users' interest in it. The latter are mainly interested in the product or service being user-friendly, with no increase to their mental load. To put it in today's terms, it is probable that compared to the Christian product, Judaism's positioning on the market of ideas was "handicapped" by its "613 rules" codified throughout the religion's history.

From the year 70 onwards, this apologetic competition between the different groups of actors in the cities in Judea and all around the Mediterranean, from the Middle East to Gaul, would unfold via very different strategies, with no guarantee of survival for either of the currents.

Between a Simple Theology With Complex Rules, and Simplified Rules With a Complex Theology

The first group of actors was composed of the Orthodox Jews of the rabbinic current in the broad sense, because the narrower current that originated in Yavne and whose historical importance is disputed must be differentiated from the much broader current that Simon Claude Mimouni calls "synagogal Judaism"[24], even if the Yavne movement was probably absorbed into rabbinic Judaism later on. This first group required compliance with the Torah, the law of Moses. Members had to be circumcised and respect dietary kashrut, the Shabbat and—as we saw with Rabbi Ben Zakkai—the various religious festivals whose dates depended on the lunar calendar and marked the months and seasons.

However, as I have already mentioned, the practice of sacrificial rites was no longer required since the Temple had been destroyed. These were replaced by prayer, study of the texts and following the many rules that organized daily life. The oral Torah was fixed in writing, leading ultimately to the Talmud. Fixation in writing is a tool to exclude heterodox factions and reinforce the orthodox factions' identity, which is under threat. Both the rabbinic Jews and the Hellenistic Christians employed this strategy.

According to Simon Claude Mimouni, "Judaism has often been defined as orthopraxy [compliance with rituals and codes and thus practices] more than an orthodoxy [a belief with dogmas][25]". The rules were complex, but the theology was simple: "The Judean 'dogma'—if we can call it that—boils down to two essential affirmations: the oneness of God and the choice of Israel [...] 'Hear, O Israel: The Lord our God is one Lord' (Deut. 6:4), which would become the daily prayer of practising Jews, the *Shema Israel*, 'Hear, O Israel'[26]".

The second group of actors, which would become dominant in its Christian form after one hundred and fifty years, between the mid-second and early-fourth centuries AD, chose a much more offensive strategy involving proselytizing and simplifying the rules and rituals, thanks in particular to baptism, which secured a "one and done" purification of original sin[27]. But this came at the cost of a more complex theology regarding the nature of the one God in three persons, the practice of the Eucharist—in which "the bread and wine are declared the body and blood of Christ[28]", i.e. the deity is incarnated in a symbolic or realistic form—and a greater emphasis on the resurrection of the dead than the Pharisees had.

To achieve its goal, this group fixed the oral message of Jesus in writing and used the letters of Paul and Peter and the Acts of the Apostles as a means of fixing the movement's origins. This set of documents later became known as the New Testament in contrast to the Torah, which for Christians represents the Old Testament, the Old Covenant with God.

The differentiation between the Jewish and Christian movements produced a result that neither the polytheistic Romans nor the rabbinic Jews expected: the victory of those who were starting to be known as Christians. Around 80 AD, the term *christianos* (Χριστιανός) referred to those who followed Christ, from *Christos* (Χριστός) in Greek, that is the Messiah in Hebrew. It was a pejorative term, as Frédéric Lenoir[29] reminds us.

This victory was unexpected given the small number of people who followed Jesus until the middle of the second century AD. It is probable that the Christian movement's expansion was helped by the Roman–Jewish wars: the Zealots' revolt of 70 AD, which opened an initial window of opportunity for the Hellenistic Christian Jews; then the Bar-Kokhba revolt of 132–135 AD that led to the near total destruction of Jerusalem.

Frédéric Lenoir attributes the strength of the emerging Christian world to the organization of what modern historians call the "Great Church", which encompassed Christians with Hellenistic origins, the "small" Church being for the Christians of Judean origin[30]. This term is taken from an anti-Christian text by "a pagan philosopher, Celsus [...] Thanks to its authority structures based on the bishop-priest hierarchy, the Great Church would define criteria for orthodoxy and at the same time relegate groups that contested these criteria to the status of heretic[31]".

The Christians of Greek origin, of the "Great Church", partly adopted the same strategy as the first rabbis of Yavne, whose goal was to define orthodoxy and then eliminate any who opposed it so as to form a more cohesive group in the face of Roman power, while at the same time seeking an alliance with the Romans.

*

Strengthening group identity by defining an orthodox belief, building on existing social networks, seeking alliances with dominant groups, stigmatizing opponents, and capturing the funding flows the project needs to succeed are all the basic mechanisms for the dissemination of any innovation, then as now. After the Temple was destroyed, the Yavne rabbis tried to collect the tithe previously collected by the Temple priests[32], something the Christians managed to do in the fourth century, according to Peter Brown.

This unexpected victory of the Christians is also characteristic of innovation processes where, as I have already pointed out, those in a dominant position struggle to identify which if any of the future start-ups might be a threat to them. One technique today is to buy them out, either to benefit from their innovative potential or to neutralize them. Emperor Constantine applied this integration strategy one hundred and fifty years later.

The Christian innovation developed even more after the fourth century as the Western Roman Empire began to slowly collapse. The Christian Church was integrated into the imperial organization, but not without transforming it, as Peter Brown points out in his book on the formation of Christianity. A clear indicator of the shifting power relations "between church and city", which was the fundamental unit of the empire, is the struggle for control of the expenditure of the Roman state. The map of Roman cities in the western Mediterranean in 400 AD shows that they were very dense[33]. They provided the bases for the diocese, just as the synagogues in these exact same cities had been the bases for Christian communities. Peter Brown quotes the historian Arnaldo Momigliano's summary of the situation around the fourth century, at the time of Augustine of Hippo (Algeria): "Money which would have gone to the building of a theatre or an aqueduct now went to the building of churches and monasteries[34]".

Anyone who has worked for a large corporation is familiar with these internal battles for budget allocation between the different departments within the organization. This is why one key and often-overlooked figure is the management controller, one of the arbiters of fiscal balance and company investment. The winner is often the actor with the best network within the organization. In the late 1960s, Alain Cottereau used the term "Panurge point" to describe the moment when everyone joins in with the collective action, when there is no way of knowing when the decision was made, only that it has been made. The shift in allocation of the Roman Empire's budget is a clear sign that the world had changed.

Chapter 9

How the Instability of the Roman Empire Favoured the Christian Innovation

The Christians' victory took time. Christianity clashed head-on with polytheistic practice, which sought out equivalences between deities, such as between Zeus and Jupiter or between Hera and Juno, rather than to impose a single "true" deity. Polytheism follows the principle of *interpretatio*, an ability to "create integration and fusion, not separation, between two different religious systems"[1]. Seeking equivalence does not mean abandoning one's identity. It allowed all the diverse deities of the Greco-Roman cities to co-exist. Polytheism is favourable to the *Cohabitation of the Gods*, to use the title of Anne-Sophie Lamine's excellent book[2]. Among all the deities, polytheistic culture will choose the one that will be the most effective at solving the problems of daily life.

Michel Piclin, for example, reports that "Plotinus was not afraid to compare Intelligence [an essential and self-sustaining substance of the One] to Saturn [Cronus for the Greeks], who, by castrating his Father, created a division in the One[3]". Conversely, it seems difficult to imagine a comparison in the Christian canon of the time between Satan and Hades, the god of the Underworld, even if some authors such as Justin, who wrote *Dialogue with Trypho*, tried to make comparisons. In another context, it is Satan himself who is the object of equivalences, as shown in the text of Zohar Hadromi-Allouche. She shows the link made in the Koran between Satan and female fertility in relation to Eve, following her expulsion from Paradise, and Demeter, the goddess of fertility in the "non-monotheistic tradition". In this particular comparison, Satan is positive[4]. This is another kind of equivalence.

Monotheism and Polytheism in Conflict

The monotheistic innovation made specific use of writing, said to express the word of God: "The *litteratura* [writing] used by God was thus not merely a tool for communication or doctrine, but a method within a universal legal case that should lead to the most supreme of conclusions: 'that He is the only God, that everything was created by Him, that He gave form to man from the earth'". These are the words of Tertullian, a late-second-century-AD Christian theologian from Carthage (Tunisia), cited by Maurizio Bettini[5].

Tertullian was an important promoter of change in polytheistic religious practices, which are based on immanent practices such as dreams, visions and looking for signs in the entrails of animals. He advocated transforming them into transcendent monotheistic practices based on evidence, argument, truth and a single God. He was in continuity with the God of Judaism who declares: "I am the Lord your God, who brought you out of the land of Egypt, out of the house of slavery; you shall have no other gods before me. You shall not make for yourself an idol [...] You shall not bow down to them or worship them; for I the Lord your God am a jealous God [...]" (Ex. 20:1–5)[6]. Jewish and then Christian monotheism rejected polytheism outright.

However, originally, this one and only true God may not have been so jealous. Nissim Amzallag proposes a realistic, not symbolic, interpretation of the term "jealous"[7]. He sees it as a metaphorical translation of the ancient Hebrew word *qanna*, which does not mean that God is jealous, but that he possesses the power to regenerate "matter by destroying form", like the blacksmith of whom Yahweh is the god. God, it would seem, was not jealous. On the contrary, he had the ability to revitalize the world. In the 11th century BC, in the kingdom of Israel ruled by King David, the polytheistic culture of magico-religious efficiency was still very much present.

As Maurizio Bettini writes, in the polytheistic world, God does not speak through writing: "The gods did not speak of themselves, it was men who spoke of them[8]". In her book *Histoire des mythes grecs*, Pauline Schmitt Pantel confirms that it was the poets, inspired by the deities, the Muses, who created the myths for public oral recitation[9]. Maurizio Bettini adds: "A god who expresses himself in writing constitutes a major cultural mutation [...] In the Christian world (as would also be the case later on in the Islamic world), God has become the 'author' of the book about himself[10]". This "author God" constitutes a truly disruptive innovation in the polytheistic world.

This observation reminds us that an innovation can be qualified as disruptive not only in relation to what preceded it, but also, and above all, in relation to the receiving context that it is entering. A disruptive innovation is not just a new "technology" or a new service. It is innovative if it also disrupts everyday customs and practices or even social relations, be they in terms of class, gender, generation or culture.

The term polytheism, in the sense of a religion with many gods, did not appear until the first century AD with Philo, a Hellenistic Jewish philosopher in Alexandria. Zohar Hadromi-Allouche, a specialist in Islam, uses the term "non-monotheistic tradition[11]" instead. As for the term monotheist, it was coined much later and in a very different context, by "an eighteenth-century English theologian Henry More[12]". These categories are therefore relative and should only be used as approximations to describe belief-based practices or differences in cultural viewpoints and without value judgements.

All this debate about the written word and the role of sacred texts, and therefore of religion, may seem superfluous now that we have forgotten the flexibility of polytheism. The historian Vinciane Pirenne-Delforge confirms that Greek religion "as a polytheistic system [was] a fundamentally plural, flexible and adaptable whole[13]".

On the other hand, polytheism can be relatively inflexible towards monotheism if it perceives it as a threat to the city. Just remember what happened in the second century BC when King Antiochus IV sought to impose an altar dedicated to Zeus (Ζεύς) in the Temple of Jerusalem. The refusal of the seven brothers and their mother to comply cost them dearly. The emperors and some of the Roman people were also wary of these monotheistic "superstitions". This also explains why polytheistic cults survived well beyond the fourth century in a world that had become increasingly Christian yet remained steeped in polytheism.

As a disruption, taking a sacred book to be the word of God was on a par with the shift from monastic scribes to the printing press in the fifteenth century, or from biofuels to fossil fuels in the eighteenth century and from paper to digital communication in the twenty-first century.

Peter Drucker (1909–2005), one of the inventors of modern management, used an interesting shortcut to show the unforeseeable link between the invention of printing by Gutenberg (c. 1400–1468) and the invention of capitalism in the nineteenth century. Thanks to the printing press, books could be produced in multiple copies, which in turn made them cheaper and thus made the Bible accessible to a wider audience. This led to the development of Protestantism and thus to the birth of capitalism, as the great German sociologist Max Weber demonstrated in his 1905 book *The Protestant Ethic and the Spirit of Capitalism*. Peter Drucker's point is that predicting the future uses of a technical invention cannot be done by looking at its qualities but by looking at the uses that emerge throughout its reception process[14].

The permanence of "old technologies", such as polytheism, is a frequent phenomenon in innovation processes. The arrival of the Internet did not cause paper to disappear, unlike the fax and the Paris pneumatic post, which did succumb. A practice can survive for a long time after the emergence of a dominant innovation. It can even be reinterpreted and reborn with another use, as with film photography or vinyl records.

The Organization of Christian Churches: How to Exclude Heretics and Strengthen Communities

From the late first century onwards, some historical sources on the spread of what would become Christianity, especially in the East, are not available: "It takes a shrewd mind to say how the Gospel spread in Egypt, Arabia, Mesopotamia and in the Persian Empire, India or Armenia during the first five centuries[15]." The historian Simon Claude Mimouni confirms that "we know less about the second century than about the first century, at least from the standpoint of literary documentation, and this is despite the relatively abundant discoveries for this period in epigraphy and papyrology[16]".

As is often the case in history, what seems clear today—the distinction between Jews and Christians—was not at all clear in the late first century AD and beyond. Karen King, quoted by Adriana Destro and Mauro Pesce of the University of Bologna, recalls that at the beginning of Christian Judaism nothing was fixed, "no fixed canon, creed, or ritual, no established institutions or hierarchy of bishops and laity, no church buildings or sacred art". It was a "story fraught with conflict and controversy[17]". The term Christianity, an attempt to integrate both the human and divine dimensions of Jesus, only appeared in the early second

The Organization of Christian Churches

century, in Syria, in the writings of the bishop Ignatius of Antioch[18] (c. 35–107/113). He is considered one of the first Church Fathers.

In order to grasp the next stages of the innovation process, at least the expansion phase between the first and fourth centuries, we must understand that the religious power of the Jesus movement gradually shifted from Jerusalem to Rome, and then from the synagogues to the Christian churches[19].

At the end of the first century, the power of the churches was highly decentralized: "In Rome as in Corinth there was a collegial leadership of presbyters or episcopi" who would later become bishops. They were considered to be the successors of the apostles, as Gérard Mordillat and Jérôme Prieur remind us when they quote Irenaeus of Lyons, another important Church Father: "Obey those presbyters in the church, who have succession [...] from the apostles; who, with the succession of the episcopate, received the gift of truth, according to the good pleasure of the Father[20]."

Collegial leadership disappeared in the second century[21] to be replaced by the bishop in Rome. Like the synagogues, all these churches, which were linked to the networks of Roman, Greek and Middle Eastern cities, formed a key social network for the spread of Christianity.

According to Enrico Norelli, the success of Christianity was due not only to the proselytizing energy that the early Christians deployed with passion, but also to their charitable deeds "widely noted and celebrated, or envied, by non-Christians[22]". The geographical shift of religious power to Rome indicates that what was becoming Christianity was expanding into the heart of the Roman Empire. The Empire served as an organizational model for Christianity, which became incorporated into Roman bureaucracy by the third century AD.

Enrico Norelli makes cautious use of the previously mentioned hypothesis put forward by the sociologist of religion Rodney Stark concerning the growth of the Christian population between the years 40 and 310, shortly before the conversion of Emperor Constantine. He assumes that shortly after his death, Jesus had around a thousand believers. Two hundred and fifty years later, there may have been nearly 9 million. However, he points out that "this is purely a hypothesis[23]". Nonetheless, this indicates that the number of actors involved in Christianity had become very large, although the sources are scarcer. Most of what remains are debates about how to define the belief.

The Proliferation of Currents Embracing Jesus

For two and a half centuries, numerous theories influenced by the East and by Greek philosophy emerged in the Roman world. The wealthy shipowner Marcion (85–160) defended "the existence of two deities: a lower, creator god and a higher, saviour god; the former was known through Moses and the latter remained unknown, only to be revealed in Christ[24]". He eventually left the Church and founded his own community. Another figure in the 140s in Rome, Valentinus, spoke of a "new knowledge", "gnosis", for which "the world is evil and man unhappy"[25]. In the third century, a new actor by the name of Mani (c. 216–274), the father of Manichaeism, appeared. He came from Babylonia: "Most of his writings [are] in Syriac, which was the dominant literary language in third-century Mesopotamia." The Manichaeans practised "neither baptism nor the Eucharist[26]". Mani would remain outside Christianity, but not without influencing it from the margins. All this constituted a tumultuous intellectual and religious world abuzz with multiple debates.

There were other currents that questioned the identity of Jesus more directly. All throughout the first and second centuries, docetism denied that Jesus was flesh-and-blood, because "he is solely God[27]". The Church Fathers defended the idea of Jesus as both Christ and God. They developed the idea of a single God in three persons: Father, Son and Holy Spirit. They retained the monotheism of Judaism, but added a dual nature, both human and divine, while rejecting all the different forms of dualism that sought to separate Jesus' divine nature from his human nature[28]. The idea of a single God is perhaps close to Plotinus' concept of the One mentioned above.

These debates led to a serious crisis for Christianity in the fourth century: Arianism, named after Arius (c. 250–336), a priest from near Alexandria. He refused to accept Christ as equal to God: "Arius therefore places Christ in a subordinate position, as a second in command, a God incarnated and imperfect by nature, since the Father alone is eternal [...] the Father and the Son are not of the same substance or essence, they are not consubstantial[29]." He was condemned for heresy in Egypt in 319 by the bishop Alexander of Alexandria.

Irenaeus, the bishop of Lyons (c. 130–c. 202), who I have already mentioned, was to play a major role in establishing Christian orthodoxy around 180 AD[30]. Christian orthodoxy was written in parallel to Jewish orthodoxy, which is expressed in the Mishna. As Peter Brown notes: "Jewish synagogues throughout the empire thrived in exactly the same manner [as Christian churches]."

He adds: "Church and synagogue alike provided a space where the moderately rich could shine through pious donations[31]." Peter Brown's point is that "It was the gathering pace of the entry of the rich into the Christian churches in the period after 370—and not the conversion of Constantine in 312—that marks the true beginning of the triumphant Catholicism of the Middle Ages[32]." But that is another story...

An Irreversible Fracture: The Birth of the "Deicidal People"

According to Enrico Norelli, around the year 100, the Jesus movement was represented in "two centres of major importance, Antioch [present-day Antakya, on Turkey's southern border with northern Syria] and Rome[33]". In the first century, followers of Jesus could be found in Palestine, Asia Minor, Greece, in the east and west of the Roman Empire, largely along the routes that Paul the Apostle had taken forty years earlier.

These communities were in favour of abolishing circumcision and kashrut, and called for Shabbat to be replaced by Sunday. They originally belonged to Hellenistic Jewish groups, as the specialist in Semitic culture José Costa points out[34]. They would also maintain that Jesus was resurrected, that he is Jesus Christ, that he is of divine descent in the trinitarian mode, in three persons, hence the debates mentioned above. The resurrection made the innovation more acceptable to pagans of Greek culture.

Conversely, these claims made it unacceptable for the Jews following the Torah. This explains why Pauline Christian Jews were gradually expelled from the synagogues[35]. Clearly, relations between all these communities were becoming increasingly conflictual.

Justin, the aforementioned Christian author of *Dialogue with Trypho* [a Jewish writer with whom he is conversing][36], sought to demonstrate that the Christians represented the new covenant with God and that Jesus was indeed the Messiah. He tells us that "Bar-Kokhba, the leader of the revolt of the Jews, gave orders that Christians alone should be led to cruel punishments, unless they would deny Jesus Christ and utter blasphemy[37]". Relations between the different fractions of Judaism were therefore at a low point. These conflicts contributed to the separation of the Jewish world from the Christian world[38].

Around the same time, circa 150, a Christian author and bishop, Melito of Sardis (in modern Turkey), made this separation. He was probably the first to brand the Pharisee Judeans as a "deicidal people", a term that persisted until the Second Vatican Council (1962–1965)[39]. He "sought to define a certain Christian conscience by stripping the Judean nation of this tradition [...] Melito is therefore an essential link, in the 160s, for understanding how the Christian conscience was formed in a climate of extreme conflict with the Pharisees [...] He witnessed the completion of the separation between Christians and Pharisees, at least in Anatolia [present-day Turkey][40]".

Overall, the polemic lay initially within the various trends of Judaism, hence we cannot speak of Christian anti-Judaism at that time. The Pharisee movement, the future Rabbinic Judaism, was itself split between supporters of Hillel and of Shammai, with the latter movement losing its influence later on[41]. However, towards the end of the second century, "Christians of Greek origin no longer seemed to be aware of all that they owed to Judaism, from a liturgical, exegetical and institutional point of view[42]".

From the mid-second century onwards, the population of Pagan-Christians, the Christians who were not of Jewish descent, grew and was integrated into the urban networks around the Mediterranean rim and into the organization of the Roman Empire itself. This would prove to be a long and arduous process, because the Christians were regularly persecuted for what the Roman's saw as their impiety. These attacks mainly affected the Christians in the West until the early fourth century, continuing under Diocletian in 303, just before Constantine's "conversion" in 312.

The Christians' Difficult Incorporation Into the Empire's Polytheistic Culture

The compatibility between monotheistic Christian and polytheistic beliefs remains relatively mysterious. There are, however, historical indications that show the progressive integration of Christians into the Roman political and administrative system, such as into the magistracy from 260 onwards, following the edict of toleration by the Emperor

Gallienus, and into the Roman army[43]. The movement grew further under Emperor Constantine[44].

The expansion of Christianity "in the second half of the third century was particularly significant[45]". Christians were everywhere, all around the Mediterranean, in Mesopotamia, Syria, Palestine, and as far as Arabia, Egypt, Cyrenaica (Libya), North Africa, but also in Asia Minor, Greece, Rome, Gaul, all the way to the north of the Danube and Germania[46]. The Christians with their monotheism were more or less tolerated. Relations between polytheists and monotheists would become strained whenever famine, political unrest or epidemics struck. Every time, the monotheistic cults were blamed as the source of misfortune. Christians were used as scapegoats to explain society's woes, the same model followed by conspiracy theories today. "Public opinion accused Christians of 'depravity': infanticide, cannibalism, collective debauchery and even incest, not to mention magical or bizarre practices like worshipping a donkey's head[47]." These recurring accusations were behind a whole series of persecutions against Christians, such as under the reign of emperor Decius, who was hostile to Christianity (249–250)[48], or under the emperor Valerian between 257 and 258. The harshest of all occurred between 303 and 312 under emperor Diocletian. In each case, because of their monotheism, the Christians were deemed a threat to the state and the cities, which were protected by multiple deities. Diocletian held that the Christians could not be assimilated[49]. Accusations against groups with which a portion of public opinion disagrees are strikingly consistent. Some of the accusations above are similar to QAnon taxing US Democrats with paedophilia, for example, while others are echoed in supremacist groups' claims about minorities deemed unassimilable and threatening.

A Dual Monetary and Human Energy Crisis Delivers an Opportunity for Christianity

To put it somewhat bluntly, the triumph of Christianity was the product of the Roman Empire's difficulties in controlling human energy in the third century. The Empire was a military and slave-based operation underpinned by the towns and by taxes on peasants. One third or one quarter of the population at the time are thought to have been slaves[50]. The Empire needed vast amounts of funds, as it constantly needed new resources to fund its armies protecting its borders near the great rivers on its outer edges: the Rhine, the Danube, the Tigris and the Euphrates.

The army also served to supply the slave labour needed on the large farms in Italy and probably all over North Africa, the Roman Empire's wealthiest agricultural region. The agricultural "labor force [...] amounted to over 80 percent of the overall population" during the grain harvests, which ran from spring to late summer from south to north, from the Middle East to the Rhine[51].

If slaves became scarce, their price increased and an economic crisis ensued. The role of slaves in the economic system is a reminder of how important human energy was to the functioning of societies before the coal energy revolution tipped the world's new economic order in favour of Britain and the West in the mid-18th century[52], and thereby put an end to slavery. Coal energy replaced human energy. As it happens, as Bruno Dumézil shows[53], the Roman Empire was in a permanent state of crisis from the third century, enduring civil war after civil war. Its currency became almost worthless, meaning it could no longer pay its soldiers, who were no longer capturing slaves. Slave prices went up. Taxes increased. Peasants abandoned the land. Harvests declined and tax revenues dried up. In the late third century, the emperor Diocletian introduced tax reforms that tied the peasants to the land and required the large landowners to collect tax, presaging the later Western feudal system. However, none of this was enough. This economic and monetary crisis proved to be Christianity's chance.

Constantine had just defeated his rival Maxentius in 312. Driven by a prophetic dream inspired by the Cross of Christ, he converted to Christianity, but without being baptized. The story could have ended there as nothing more than an individual conversion, as Paul Veyne suggests[54]. However, Bruno Dumézil adds another equally important historical element. Constantine launched monetary reforms, with a new currency, a gold coin called the *solidus*, the origin of the French *sou*. He found the gold in the Roman temples. "Luckily", as Bruno Dumézil says, "Constantine had access to a decent reserve of precious metals. His first act on becoming a Christian was to confiscate all the precious metals from the pagan temples. The gold pagan statues and gilded temple surfaces were all melted down to make the *solidi* to pay the soldiers[55]."

In 313, Constantine published a circular, which would be known as the "Edict of Milan". This text made Christianity a legal religion with the same status as "paganism". Placing Christianity on an equal footing with the pagan religion allowed Constantine to seize the gold from the temples, thereby allowing him to revalue the currency and gain the support of the Christian Church, which would become a kind of delegated administration. "Constantine granted to bishops and clergymen the same privileges that had always been accorded by Roman emperors to those who furthered the cultural and religious ends of Roman society", namely "pagan priests (whose exemptions Constantine maintained), professors, doctors, and the leaders of Jewish synagogues"[56].

However, they were never granted "exemption from the land tax, which was the principal tax of the empire[57]". The Christian Church would partly serve to prop up the Roman administration. The Christian problem became a solution to slow the fall of Rome. "Christianity was a religion of the city [...] By the fourth century, almost every city had its bishop, every Roman province's capital had its archbishop, every imperial capital had its patriarch[58]." The Church was in favour of the emperors. "The bishops soon realized that the success of Christianity had been assured by the Roman emperors[59]". With the Edict of Thessalonica (380), Theodosius established the Christian religion as the state religion in Constantinople, where he was based, and which had been the new capital of the Roman Empire since 330. The Church in turn recognized the emperor's power to convene councils, define what constituted true faith and to be "God's lieutenant on earth". "The idea of proximity between Church and State is a Roman idea[60]". Thus, there were "three main State bodies": the Church, the civil service and the army[61].

The Progressive Incorporation of Christians Into the Roman Establishment

All that remained for Constantine to do was to unify the various religious currents within Christianity. In 325, he gathered the bishops in Nicaea, in Asia Minor, in modern Turkey. This "Eastern" council resulted in the rejection of Arianism, which professed that Christ, the son of man in the Jewish tradition, was begotten and therefore not equivalent to the Father. The Council of Nicaea formalized, in Greek, the belief in the Trinity, where the son is consubstantial with the Father, and the symbol of the Cross, which Constantine had already used to defeat Maxentius in 312.

It established a common standard that unified the belief, thereby bolstering its spread and its hold over the "users". The establishment of a standard is an invariant in innovation processes because it facilitates the invention's collective use, circulation and "imitation", to take the term used by Gabriel Tarde in 1895[62].

Paradoxically, the recognition of Christianity did not sound the death knell for paganism. In the middle of the fourth century, the emperor Julian (361–363) even tried to reinstate paganism for two years[63]. *The City of God*, the great work by Saint Augustine of Hippo (modern Annaba, in Algeria), was published in 426 AD[64]. This book shows that tensions were still running high one hundred years after the Edict of Milan. Historian Peter Brown relates that Ambrose, an important Church Father who spoke Greek and Latin and was Bishop of Milan in the late fourth century, opposed the call of the Roman pagan elite to reinstate Imperial funding for pagan cults[65].

When Alaric's Visigoths invaded Rome in 410, the pagans accused the Christians of causing this calamity. Some experienced the Sack of Rome as the end of the world, as the destruction of the Temple in 70 had been for the Jews.

The pagan elites maintained that Rome had been protected by polytheism before the Christians arrived. Saint Augustine took it upon himself to refute this claim by showing that polytheism had never protected Rome from anything. As Philippe Cournault shows, he sought to demonstrate the superiority of Christianity[66]. The pagans' concerns were similar to those of the ancient Hebrews' "fear of change"—linked to the risk of losing their "social security"—during the transition from polytheism to monotheism around the tenth century BC. This polemic confirms that an innovation can never be taken for granted and can always disappear. Ramsey MacMullen shows that paganism lasted a long time. Even today, it may still not have disappeared. Christianity would have to make concessions and allow itself to be reinterpreted by polytheism, because, as Ramsay MacMullen writes, "ordinary human needs were answered by traditional religion[67]".

The Christians developed relatively typical strategies for establishing their religion among populations that did not spontaneously convert. They took the attacks previously directed at them and turned them against the pagans. They accused them of "heathen enormities" and resorted to "inflammatory name-calling", describing their sacrifices as "nefarious rites"[68]. They also used coercion in the early fifth century, using monks as "shock troops", as at the time of the Hasmonean conquest of Idumaea[69]. Evergetism, a form of collective investment by the wealthy Romans in favour of the people, was replaced by cronyism, with Christians occupying positions in the Roman administration that allowed them to defend their cronies' interests[70]. Christians made up the majority of imperial officials by between 360 and 370[71].

Ultimately, Christianity allowed pagan practices to be retained. Like Augustine, another early fifth-century Church Father, Jerome, conceded that "better, worship of saints in the pagan manner than none at all [...] In due course holy images, also, first of Jesus and John the Baptist, then of other figures, and, by preference, paintings of saints and angels decorated the walls [of churches]". Lastly, the churches responded to requests for "healing, whether mental or physical", and for "advice in one's personal crises, or punishment of the wicked". Many objects of pagan origin were preserved, such as candles, bells or holy water to protect against diseases and produce a good harvest[72]. The Swedish religious historian Martin P. Nilsson confirms that in Greece, when the sacrifice began, "a firebrand was taken from the altar and dipped in water" to "sprinkle the congregation as well as the animal to be sacrificed". "At the entrance to the temple there was a font filled with water for performing ablutions before entering[73]".

When it comes to dosing the amount of magic in the belief, the dose was much higher in the past but has not disappeared today, because the problems of everyday life are still there, but in their modern forms. As we have seen in the progressive history of the transition from polytheism to monotheism, there was never a radical split.

Miracles, wonders and magic are visible signs of the existence of the forces that govern us. The following of saints and marabouts in "sub-Saharan Islam[74]" and the Catholics' praying to saints supposed to solve everyday problems are reminders that this link is an important one. All throughout human history, many religious reformers have sought to "purify" this or that religion of its "magical" practices. The magico-religious element enchants the difficult and uncertain reality of agrarian societies. Advertising and "right-wing" or "left-wing" populism do the same for modern societies.

*

The Church did not triumph by suppressing paganism but rather by assimilating some of its practices. It also successfully mobilized a whole series of techniques for capturing "users", from persuasion to force, as in many innovation processes. Physical coercion, cronyism, social benefits, stigmatizing opponents, mobilizing elite intellectuals, a high capacity for incorporating effective pagan practices into Christian rituals, the crises of the Roman Empire—all of this explains the success of Christianity from the fourth century onwards, made even stronger and more effective by its organization into diocese established in the many cities that surrounded the Mediterranean. The conclusion is counterintuitive: as an innovation, Christianity was disruptive of beliefs but delivered a form of continuity with past practices.

~ ~ ~

Conclusion

The Diverse and Blended Course of Christian Monotheism

The stories in polytheism are of deities with similar concerns to humans. The poems recited by the *aoidos*, the "poet-singer-griot-bard[1]", speak of love, power, travels, suffering, violence and death. In monotheism, God speaks to the people. The idea of divine revelation was a disruptive innovation in the polytheistic Mediterranean world. Its development, via Judaism and then Christianity, was the result of transgressions, coercion of varying degrees of violence and numerous reinterpretations.

But when it passed from the Jewish world to the Christian world, monotheism itself underwent significant change. In three hundred years, the ancient monotheism that proclaimed the *Shema Israel* in Hebrew—"Hear, O Israel: the Lord our God, the Lord is One! [...] For you are a holy people to the Lord your God; the Lord your God has chosen you to be a people for Himself, a special treasure above all the peoples on the face of the earth[2]" (Deut. 6:4 and 7:6)—was overrun by a new, more-conquering form of monotheism.

One that first declared in Greek in 325, at Nicaea, east of Constantinople, in the eastern Roman Empire: "Πιστεύομεν εἰς ἕνα Θεόν" ("*We* believe in one God"). With the break-up of the Empire in the fifth century, Latin became dominant in the west and separated from Greek, which remained dominant around Constantinople, which later became Istanbul. Saint Augustine himself, the African Christian, did not speak Greek[3].

The Nicene Creed gradually changed from Greek to Latin and from "we" to "I":

> *I* believe in one God [...]
> *I* believe in one Lord Jesus Christ,
> the Only Begotten Son of God, born of the Father before all ages, [...]
> begotten,
> not made, *consubstantial* [i.e. being of the same substance] *with the Father*;
> [...] I believe in the *Holy Spirit*, the Lord, the giver of life, who proceeds from the *Father and the Son*, [...]
> I believe in one, holy, *catholic* and apostolic Church.
> I *confess one Baptism* for the forgiveness of sins
> and *I look forward to the resurrection of the dead*
> and the life of the world to come. Amen[4].

Amen is a Hebrew word that equates to "you bet!", as Father Robert Tamisier[5] would playfully explain to us during his exegesis classes in the 1960s. The change was from a single God to a God in three persons. The monotheism invention was transformed into a disruptive innovation organized by an expanding social group, the Christians.

To elucidate this transition from a polytheistic to a monotheistic world using an anthropological approach, we must include the agrarian system, the social system and the religious system.

Marcel Mauss' study of the Eskimos, published in 1904–1905, is the epitome of anthropological analysis. It combines material, social and symbolic elements, much like Bronislaw Malinowski's study of the Trobrianders, *Argonauts of the Western Pacific*, published in 1922[6]. To explain how society functions as a "total social phenomenon", to use Mauss' central concept in *The Gift*, first published in 1923–1924 in *L'Année Sociologique*[7], he mobilizes technical objects, the climate and seasons, family and religion (as in Madagascar at the time of Andrianampoinimerina), but not in a global approach, i.e. at all scales of observation at once, which is impossible[8].

The anthropological reconstruction of the spread of Christianity clearly reveals the three main stages that can be found in most innovation processes in both the past and present. The first stage is the invention: Jesus. It is more individual, backed by a very small group, of uncertain origin and with multiple competitors. Everything is vague. Everything is fragile. Everything is in turmoil. Nothing is certain. The second stage is the innovation. It is more collective. It shows how the interplay of actors within their own organization and the system of action in which they find themselves favour the aggregation and therefore the reinterpretation of multiple inventions, which in turn leads to either the disappearance or spread of the innovation. The mobilizing figure or figures such as Paul the Apostle play a driving role in this dynamic. The third stage is reception. It is often triggered by a climate, monetary or politico-military crisis that changes the balance of power by ushering in a new alliance among existing and emerging social groups. The crisis opens a window of opportunity that is limited in time. It provides an opportunity for the innovation, in this case the Christian monotheism of a God in three persons, to develop.

At the same time, in a nonlinear manner and without any pre-established order of entering the maelstrom, this diffusion mobilizes a whirlwind of multifaceted causalities: the material, logistical, climatic, energy, budgetary, military, social, linguistic and symbolic dimensions[9].

By transforming Jesus into a deity equivalent to the Father, and thus to the one God, the Council of Nicaea confirmed the shift from the incremental invention launched by Jesus in an effort to reform Judaism in the early first century, to a disruptive innovation that would marginalize rabbinic Judaism and cause Greco-Roman polytheism to disappear, at least in its institutional form, although in practice it would continue among the converted pagan populations. The diffusion of a disruptive innovation requires both continuity and discontinuity in its uses, as Christianity shows.

Postscript: An Aid to Understanding Today's Innovation Processes

There's a Jewish joke that says God often rereads the Torah to try to understand what's going on in this world he created.

(Hervé Le Tellier, *The Anomaly*, 2021, Other Press)

The core business of anthropology is about solving puzzles. Here, the meaning, interests and conflictual origins of innovations or changes are the puzzle. The puzzle begins with an observation: something or someone is out of the ordinary or uncommon. From this point of view, all anthropological studies take place in exotic worlds, universes of difference, irrespective of whether they belong to the past, the present or the future, whether they are in France, China, Africa, Brazil or the United States, or whether the topic is disability or high net worth.

This is why only what is true exists, only pieces of truth. All truths are ambivalent. They are not only positive or negative, but also multifaceted. Presenting the birth of Jewish and then Christian monotheism as a puzzle to be solved in order to understand the social, material and symbolic logics underlying the process of its emergence only shows one facet of the reality. Anthropology does not exhaustively describe and interpret this innovation. And yet, every time we frame reality through a scope, a *découpage*, if it is done methodically, truth is revealed.

A *découpage* is true not because it is coherent—paranoid conspiracy theories are hyper-coherent whereas reality is heterogeneous and contradictory; nor because it is based on frequencies, series or correlations, which are statistical or experimental methods external to the situations and their dynamics, i.e. outside the interplay of actors; nor because it is global; but because it describes *some* reality, the reality of the power relations between social actors under the constraint of the historical configurations in which their social interactions are embedded. To analyze the reality, this approach does not start from what the rules, faith, belief or moral standards contain, but from the power relations, alliances, survival constraints, tensions or threats that act as triggers for the interplay of actors.

This strategic anthropological *découpage* focuses on the practices and uses of a novelty. It reveals that innovation processes fall simultaneously within a configuration effect, an actor effect and an unpredictable "black swan" effect. When all three dimensions align, rather like the planets for some, conditions are favourable for innovations to emerge. This alignment therefore corresponds to a window of opportunity linked to the course of things, the *shi* (势) in Chinese, an opening that allows the innovation to spread. The problem for social actors is that this alignment is not always visible.

One of the methodological conclusions I drew from this is that it is not possible to observe all the links between these different effects at the same time, because there is no observation without a *découpage*, without a scale of observation[1]. Strategic anthropology can be "total" when it incorporates the material, social and symbolic, but it is not "global", i.e. going from micro to macro, from genetics to geopolitics, from geology to space. In this approach, the individual may believe themself to be the centre of the world but they are not central. This is an inductive approach that models, that interprets the observed phenomena at the end of the investigation and not at the beginning. As a model, it is one of "limited generalization"[2].

The Invariants, From Ancient Palestine to 21st Century China

Since my initial foray into solving the puzzle of why Malagasy peasants were rejecting a new technology, I have spent thirty years hunting down other puzzles. I have not done this alone. Sophie Taponier, Sophie Alami, Isabelle Garabuau-Moussaoui and many others have joined me. All these studies helped me to incrementally assemble the different stages of a general model that describes innovation processes and that can be used to describe the emergence of Babylonian, Jewish and Christian monotheism. More than once, I have felt like an archaeologist on a dig who uncovers a few inscriptions on a dish, a wall or a clay tablet. From hardly anything at all, he must reconstruct the culture and daily life of an entire era or social group.

Between 1997 and 2019, I tackled a whole series of puzzles about the diffusion of new household items in Chinese homes, from cosmetics and food products to electrical appliances, games and digital technology. Thanks to the studies I conducted with Zheng Lihua, Anne Sophie Boisard and Yang Xiaomin and their research teams, and then with Wang Lei, Hu Shen and Ma Jingjing, we were able to observe in real time the logistical, social and symbolic conditions for the diffusion of consumer goods.

In the late 1990s, there were very few products in Chinese bathrooms. For the father, mother and only child, there would be three towels, three toothbrushes, one bottle of shampoo and one bar of soap. In 2018, the Chinese middle class had fitted kitchens and cupboards and shelves in their bathrooms containing dozens of beauty products, creams, lotions and make-up.

In the meantime, the entire urban and domestic logistics system had undergone a similar transformation to that seen in Western Europe between 1945 and 1975, and in the United States in the 1920s. Newly built road infrastructure facilitated the supply of the mass retail sector that was established in the mid-2000s. Mobility evolved thanks to underground rail, high-speed trains and cars, allowing organized flows among homes, work places and shopping areas. Rural populations migrated en masse to the cities, accelerating the construction of apartment buildings.

Within the home, domestic infrastructure—running water and electricity—became mainstream. This allowed the use of kitchen appliances such as refrigerators, cookers, microwave ovens and bottle sterilizers. Hot-water boilers were installed in bathrooms. Then came the communication devices: colour televisions, Internet connections, computers, mobile phones and tablets, which allowed the development of e-commerce, electronic payment and digital currency.

At the same time, there were more divorces, which completely transformed the way the marriage market functioned and changed women's relationships to their bodies, which became an asset that had to be maintained in order to find a new husband in the event of divorce. This lifestyle change opened up the market for cosmetic products. Cosmetics themselves were reinterpreted around the particularity of Chinese social interactions, which deal in face (*miànzi*, 面子). Valuing one's body means valuing one's group and "gaining face". The incoming innovations (new household appliances, beauty treatments and digital communication) were determined by both logistical and lifestyle transformations among the Chinese urban middle class. From the 1990s onwards, the Chinese upper middle class adopted Western practices such as home appliances, ready-meals, processed beverages and cars.

The configuration in place at the time of the Hellenization of Palestine is the model that most closely resembles the introduction of new consumer goods in China. The Judeans began by incorporating numerous foreign practices: the stadia and the questioning of circumcision by the upper class in Palestine in the second century BC. Hellenization would create a common space thanks to *koinè*, Greek, which served as lingua franca for the dissemination of goods and of ideas. In the Mediterranean, the *Pax Romana* favoured the circulation of goods and people, thus creating the logistical conditions for the spread of monotheism, first Jewish and then Christian, from the second century AD. The logistical system for the distribution of religious ideas was initially the pagan temples, and then later the synagogues. Operating from these hubs, these "religious platforms", the system favoured the development of the Christian churches[3].

Understanding this configuration is a way to solve the puzzle of the spread of innovations such as Jewish monotheism and then Christianity. Christianity transformed Judaism and was in turn transformed by paganism. It developed thanks to the establishment of a system of distribution platforms for ideas that competed with those of the Jews and pagans until the fourth century AD, before a new wave arrived in the seventh century with Islam and the mosques.

The Innovation Process Is Organized by the Interaction of Possibilities and Constraints

An invention can only spread if a certain number of logistical and social conditions are already in place at the time of its expansion. These are the result of triggering events that may be biological, microbial[4], climatic, energetic, material, logistical, geographical, agricultural, military, monetary, tax-related, linked to "pre-digital" social networks, linguistic, cultural or symbolic. They help the innovation progress through the different stages, and the absence of one element can block the whole process. These different elements are not all visible at the same time, and the historian Kyle Harper reminds us that discovering them depends on the choice of focal point and hence on the scales of observation[5].

In 1994, we conducted a study to understand the mechanisms behind the diffusion of Geographic Information Systems (GISs)—which in a way are the "ancestors" of big data—among agricultural professionals who seemed reluctant to adopt them. To solve the puzzle, we needed to take a detour. It was not enough to focus on the technical content, nor on the supposedly inadequate training, nor on the communication meant to demonstrate the benefits of the new technology, nor on the loss of values brought about by the change. We also had to explore the constraints that came with its use.

Twenty-five years later, the answer seems simple, but in the early 1990s things were not so clear. GISs were costly, learning to use them took time and they were slow, all of which made them very complex to use. When the acquisition cost is high, the learning curve is long and the innovation does not save time, it is unlikely to spread[6].

In the case of Christianity, it spread partly thanks to the simplification of religious rules, in contrast to Judaism, with the removal of kashrut and circumcision and the reduction of purification rituals to one action, baptism. It is as if Christianity had succeeded in lowering believers' mental load with regard to religious rules. It did however have to make concessions towards pagan practices that significantly reassured the Roman population about the uncertainties of everyday life, otherwise Christianity would have increased the new Christians' mental load and anxiety, which in turn would have fuelled an already existing movement calling for its rejection. Hence, part of their rituals were incorporated.

In another international study in 1999, we looked at the conditions for changing practices linked to a Hewlett-Packard calculator. Working with Bernard Cova in management sciences and the Argonautes team[7], we showed that it was difficult to change users' practices, because this calculator carried a strong identity load. Changing calculator meant a change of professional identity and even lowering the quality of work. The question of identity in innovation processes is often not very visible. It organizes opposition to or acceptance of invention in a clandestine way. Part of the opposition to technical or organizational innovation is due to the fear of losing one's identity, which some of the actors experience as a threat. The simplification of rules offered by Christianity threatened the religious and ethnic identity of the first-century Jews, hence their opposition. On the other hand, it made the Jewish religion less threatening for some of the Greeks.

In another context in the mid-1990s, we were faced with another puzzle at the French Ministry of Public Works. We were asked to explain why the IT staff, who had been enthusiastic about the introduction of Microsoft Word 2.0, were much less in favour of the introduction of Word 6.0. Our study showed that those members of the IT staff who had just spent considerable energy confronting strong inertia and reluctance from their department were tired and did not have the energy to return to battle and go through more discomfort. On the other hand, those who had not mobilized when Microsoft Word 2.0 arrived did so for the switch to Word 6.0, thus benefiting from an upgrade of their IT systems. In reality, things were much more complex, but this case reveals a dimension that is often overlooked, namely the amount of human energy that change-makers are prepared to spend. To grasp the importance of human energy in change processes, we need only think of start-up entrepreneurs, for example, or of hospitals one year into the COVID-19 pandemic, between 2020 and 2021[8].

When we look at the emergence of Christianity, according to historians, the Christian Jews and Pagan Christians appear to have spent much more energy spreading the new religious model than did the Judeans, who despite being proselytizers were less "proactive".

In 2001, when e-commerce was only just beginning to emerge, Fabrice Clochard and I worked on the development of mail-order sales[9]. In 1999, only 3 % of French people were using e-commerce and it seemed to us that mail order would spread without much difficulty. In reality, it had many invisible handicaps, especially among the working class, where most households did not own a computer and did not have an Internet connection, and some were afraid of online payments. In addition, the "last metre" problem, which is one of the logistical issues in delivery, was a further obstacle because most mailboxes were too small for some of the parcels. Lastly, mail-order companies had much higher overheads than the new e-commerce players, which had very few employees and low warehousing and rental costs. Mail order was overtaken by the online platforms, like Judaism was by Christianity, and took a long time to adapt to the new digital socio-economic system.

The Polytheistic Model: A Cumulative Method That Looks for Equivalences

By choosing to observe the dual religious innovation of Jewish monotheism and then Christianity, we can enrich the fields of the sociology and anthropology of innovation[10], of science and technology[11] and of decision-making processes. Most often, the topic of innovation evokes organizations[12], businesses, research laboratories[13], hospitals, non-profits and NGOs, markets[14] or how a product or service is received by consumers[15] or by companies.

The strategic anthropology approach seems to me to have some similarities to the polytheistic model. It is centred on problem solving. It observes reality in an effort to identify the most effective models to explain it and take better action. It is inductive. In contrast to monotheism, polytheism recognizes the existence of an assortment of deities, much like the assortment of occurrences, practices or interplays among actors that the inductive method seeks out. The search for regularity and the "generality of diversity" in human behaviour is the opposite of the search for long series that minimize diversity and the unforeseen emergence of black swans.

With induction, we are able to observe what emerges and how actors reorganize the functioning of their society, organization or family during and after the crisis, as they face a new situation and the prospect of an unpredictable future. Series allow us to understand human behaviour during times of relative stability. The induction model is the reverse of explaining human behaviour by statistical frequencies. It allows us to look for the unexpected behind the invariant.

However, we must be careful not to view this difference as a value judgement in favour of induction and against the search for series, as a typical "monotheistic researcher" would do. Induction, like the polytheism for which it is a metaphor, is inclusive[16] while also preserving the methodological and explanatory differences specific to each approach. This is not to say that induction is not combative, or even aggressive. The Romans may have been polytheists but they were not kind to monotheistic beliefs. They destroyed the Temple in Jerusalem. No approach prevents conflict in society. There is no supreme paganism nor apocalyptic monotheism[17].

As an inclusive method, strategic anthropology looks for the equivalences among different theories and according to the empirical scales of observation from which they were developed. It seems to me that in descriptive terms, there are commonalities among the system of action concept used in the sociology of organizations, the field concept used by Pierre Bourdieu and that of arena in the actor-network theory. One of the criteria of equivalence is that it is perfectly possible to use the data collected via any one of these interpretative models to perform a new cumulative analysis. There is simultaneously an equivalence of descriptions, a difference of focus on one dimension of human reality rather than another, and a divergence of interpretations.

The idea of controversy found in the actor–network theory is fairly close to that of power relations, just as material culture[18] is to the non-human object, cooperation strategy is to *intéressement*, reinterpretation is to translation and the actor-network is to the total social phenomenon. There is also something resembling a link between animist "vitalist" approaches based on the energy of natural objects and that of non-human actors interacting with humans. All of this was already debated in the 1990s.

How the Analysis of the Religious Innovation Process Can Help Enrich Theories of Innovation

Analyzing the innovation process of the emergence of Christianity helped me to clarify a number of observed mechanisms, such as "causality without substance", which describes objects not as actors but as media for human action.

When studying the reception of innovations into domestic spaces, observing the system of physical objects required for the new item entering the home to function allows us to understand the chances of success or failure of this introduction. The refrigerator, cooker, pots and pans, cutlery, plates and sink constitute a system of physical objects necessary for the practice of food consumption. If one of these objects is missing, it can cause the system to malfunction. Their causality is without substance.

Conversely, germs, electrical energy, water or temperature linked to global warming act on human behaviour. They are operators of action. Theirs is a biological or energetic "causality with substance"[19].

The term "incoming innovation" offers a better description of the hidden dimension of innovation processes, which often tend to be limited to "design innovation" without taking account of the constraints on the actors who will have to use this new technology, service or religion. This permanent interaction between design and reception explains the importance of the mechanism of continuous reinterpretation of the original invention until its end use.

The term "systemic crisis", from the destruction of the Temple of Jerusalem to the COVID-19 pandemic and global warming, shows the importance of triggering events that human actors had not factored in, and whose importance varies according to historical configurations.

Between the idea and the action[20], there is the interplay of actors driven by "mobilizing figures" such as Paul the Apostle, who reinterpret the original message to address the problems to be solved in the society where it is spreading. These problems are uncertain and unpredictable, as shown by the success of Christianity between the sixth and seventh century AD, despite the plague of Justinian (541–767) and the Little Ice Age, which combined to submerge the Western Roman Empire but left the organized institution of Christianity still standing[21].

This interplay of actors explains why there is probably no such thing as a disruptive innovation that appears all of a sudden. More often than not, a disruptive innovation is the result of a whole series of incremental—i.e. progressive—inventions that are more or less independent of each other. The accumulation of incremental innovations and their unexpected aggregation depending on the new uses that emerge in society will gradually produce a break from the older cultural, political or technological systems that pre-dated them.

However, not all innovations are syncretic. They may emerge in parallel, and at odds with older beliefs, practices or technologies, until they replace them. Historically, a change in energy regime is often what triggers the emergence of an innovation. Guns are not the continuation of the bow and arrow. It took the Chinese invention of a new energy, gunpowder, in the ninth century AD for the gun to develop. Today, the transition to sustainable development is heavily dependent on a change of energy regime, from fossil fuels to renewable energy. Disruptive innovation is as much the result of a series of continuities as of discontinuities.

*

For disruptive innovation to exist, there must be a voluntary or involuntary aggregation of inventions and changes in practices or beliefs. From this anthropological perspective, a new technology without a change in society is not a disruptive innovation. Disruption is not only technical. It encompasses the technical, energy, social and symbolic dimensions. The disruption lies as much in its effects on society as in the invention itself.

A disruption cannot be decreed, because it is often the result of an aggregation of uses or ideas that the inventor did not foresee. It is also the result of seeking a monopoly and thus to eliminate its opponents, as Christianity tried to do with Judaism, especially from the fourth century AD, and as Judaism also tried to do between the first and second century AD by opposing those who followed Jesus. This is much the same strategy of tension that we see mobilized today between the American GAFAM (Google, Apple, Facebook, Amazon and Microsoft) and the Chinese BHATX (Baidu, Huawei, Alibaba, Tencent and Xiaomi).

Setting aside any matters of theology and belief, the invention of monotheism highlights certain anthropological invariants. This is therefore an agnostic analysis, neither atheistic nor religious. It respects believers, because there is no society without beliefs because there is no social life without meaning. Because the wind blows where it wishes, according to the Gospel of Saint John (John 3:8), it could very well have followed the human and non-human pathways of monotheistic innovation.

~ ~ ~

Notes

Introduction

1. Conventionally, it is more correct to write the Gospel "according to" Matthew, John or Luke, because no one is sure of the actual author.
2. Rakoto Ramiarantsoa (1995, p. 177 onwards).
3. Desjeux (1971–1975 and 1979).
4. Rakoto Ramiarantsoa (1995, p. 177 onwards).
5. Horvilleur (2020, p. 17).
6. Rocher (1968).
7. See Schmitt Pantel (2015) for a scientific analysis of myths; Pedrola and Potard (2018) for more-accessible and somewhat abridged versions.

Chapter 1
The anthropology of innovation applied to religious phenomena

1. See Desjeux (2018a, chapter 17, "Témoignage d'un réformiste de gauche sur Mai 68 à Nanterre en France").
2. See Finkelstein Israël and Römer Thomas (2019), *Aux origines de la Torah*, Paris, Bayard, p. 16.
3. See Dupont (2005) on the comparisons between Homer and Dallas as popular cultures.
4. Hu and Desjeux Dominique (2014).
5. Akrich, Callon and Latour (1988).
6. Dogan and Pahre (1991).
7. Nilsson (1955, p. 16) in French [Translator's note: this is a free translation from the French version].
8. Marc Augé (1982, p. 78) talks of polytheisms' "virtue of tolerance".
9. Bettini (2023).
10. Vesperini (2019, p. 107).
11. Clayton M. Christensen (2000).
12. See Caron (2010).
13. Liverani Mario (2020 [2003]).
14. Jauss (1990).
15. Nodet (2020, location 4530).
16. Jerphagnon (2010, p. 31).

17 Nilsson (1955, p. 134 et seq.), in French.
18 Desjeux, Alami and Taponier (1998, chapter 3).
19 MacMullen (1997, p. 158). See also the collective work under the direction of Gisel Pierre and Emery Gilles (2001), *Le christianisme est-il un monothéisme?*, Labor et Fides.
20 Desjeux, Monjaret and Taponier (1998, chap. VIII, "Sur les rites comme moyen de passage à l'action").
21 Boileau-Narcejac (1964, pp. 67 and 89).
22 Bettini (2023).
23 Bettini (2023).
24 I have also tried to use the most neutral terms possible from an anthropological perspective. The terms before Christ (BC) and Anno Domini (AD) and Before the Common Era (BCE) and Common Era (CE) are equivalent here. Likewise for the use of the term 'saint' before Paul, Peter and James. Paul the Apostle and Saint Paul are equivalent in this text. We need only accept the fact that most religious terms are trapped by each person's individual beliefs, but that each usage is respectable in a given context.
25 See Prieur and Mordillat (2004a). One of the great benefits of this series was discovering researchers from a very diverse range of historical religious currents, allowing me to then search in their texts for the historical sources of Christian innovation. It raised some very interesting controversies.

Chapter 2

Mesopotamia, the matrix of Jewish monotheism in a polytheistic world (12th to 5th centuries BC)

1 Nilsson (1955, p. 18) in French [Translator's note: this is a free translation from the French version]
2 Clévenot (1976, p. 16). The author postulates that the kingdom's unification and the establishment of monotheism were linked.
3 Barnavi (2002, p. 15).
4 Liverani Mario (2020), p. 107.
5 Finkelstein Israël, Römer Thomas (2019), pp. 46, 53, 141, 163.
6 Boissière (2020).
7 Boileau-Narcejac (1964, p. 75). The book by these two authors is an example of the inductive method (see pp. 20–21); Pierre Bayard's book *Who Killed Roger Ackroyd?* (The New Press, 2000) could equally be titled *Rewriting the Puzzle*, just as I am trying to do here with monotheism.
8 See Amzallag (2020). This account is taken from this book, which I discovered thanks to Jean-Claude Ruano-Borbalan.
9 Cline (2016). The modern country names simply give the approximate locations of these historic geographical regions.

Notes

10 *Ibid.*, p. 185 et seq.
11 Amzallag (2020, location 1191).
12 *Ibid.*, location 270.
13 English translation of the Pentateuch from www.sefaria.org.
14 Laffon (2009).
15 Translator's Note: English translations of the Christian Bible are mostly taken from the New King James version.
16 Bottéro (1992, p. 258).
17 *Ibid.*, pp. 263–265.
18 Soler (2002, p. 21 et seq.).
19 Amzallag (2020).
20 English translation of the Pentateuch from www.sefaria.org.
21 Simon-Nahun (2008).
22 Desjeux (1991, chapter "La gestion nomade de l'incertitude en Afrique sahélienne", p. 37 et seq.).
23 Liverani Mario (2020, p. 73 et seq.).
24 Desjeux (1979 and 1984).
25 Cf. Ibn Khaldoun's theory on the historical logic of the barbarian invasions, as presented by Martinez-Gros Gabriel (2021) in *De l'autre côté des croisades. L'Islam entre croisés et Mongols*.
26 Brown (2012, Chapter 1, "Harvest Shocks"). This book was brought to my attention by Jean-Claude Ruano-Borbalan.
27 Desjeux (1987).
28 Nilsson (1964, p. 122).
29 Bengtsson (1954, p. 154); recommended by David Santana.
30 Nodet and Taylor (1998, p. 442). Étienne Nodet is an eminent Dominican historian and a specialist in the origins of Christianity, Flavius Josephus and the Talmud. Justin Taylor is a Marist Father and a historian who studied at the University of Cambridge in England.
31 Soler (2002, p. 12).
32 The use of quotation marks is to highlight that Clovis' status is historically problematic, as Dumézil (2015) has questioned.
33 Long (2012, p. 80). This author helped me to avoid falling into the retrospective illusion of reading the past from the standpoint of its effects on Christianity today while forgetting the Jewish matrix, as if history were linear and without unexpected bifurcations or uncertainty, which is not the case.
34 Gadja (2002, p. 617).
35 Trevisan Semi (1999).
36 Scott (2019).

Chapter 3

The Hellenization and Romanization of the Mediterranean rim

1. Marks (2007).
2. Pomeranz (2010).
3. Fagan (2017).
4. Long (2012, location 2907).
5. Harper (2017).
6. Dumézil (2013, p. 43 et seq.).
7. Harper (2017).
8. See www.science-climat-energie.be/2020/09/04/que-nous-apprend-loptimum-climatique-romain.
9. See Benoît Rossignol's preface to the French translation of Kyle Harper's book (2019); Latour (2011).
10. Gadja (2002).
11. Dumézil (2013).
12. Lemire (2016, locations 564, 576, 660 and 797).
13. Schama (2013).
14. Doan (2019).
15. Schama (2013).
16. Nodet and Taylor (1998, p. 287). The two authors' analysis of the interpenetration of Judaism and Christianity uses a very reliable method, because it involves observing rituals and practices, which are considered stable, rather than ideas or mentalities (pp. 415–416). This means that when a practice changes, we are more or less sure that there has been a real change in society, unlike ideas which are more fluid, in this case between Christianity and Judaism.
17. Rogers (1981, p. 11 ; 1st edition, 1962).
18. Tarde (2001).
19. Schama (2013, chapter 4, section III).
20. Mimouni (2012, pp. 367 and 550). Simon Claude Mimouni is one of the leading specialists in this period. I read or consulted five of his books. He seeks to objectify the presentation of Jewish and Christian history.
21. Aslan (2014 [2013]).
22. See Long (2012, p. 21, note 1); Mimouni (2004) reserves the term Judeo-Christian for those Christians of Jewish origin who continued to recognize Jesus as the Messiah after 135: the Ebionites, Nazarenes and Elcesaites.

Notes

Chapter 4

Two great debates in the Jewish world: circumcision and proselytism

1 Mimouni (2007, p. 9).
2 Schama (2013, chapter 4, section II).
3 Mimouni (2007, p. 119).
4 *Ibid.*, pp. 116–117; Collective, 1956.
5 Identity at that time was collective, as Mimouni recalls (2012, pp. 161–162). Converting was as much about integrating an ethnic group as adopting a new belief.
6 Sand (2009, p. 133). The term *Jew*, ιουδαίος in Greek, appeared in the Roman world in the third century AD to refer to people who were not of Judean descent (p. 167).
7 *Ibid.*, p. 170.
8 See Will and Orrieux (1992).
9 Schama (2013, chapter 4, section II).
10 Harper (2017).
11 Nodet and Taylor (1998, p. 288). They refer to the census of the Roman emperor Claudius in 42, which makes these figures fairly reliable.
12 Sand (2009, p. 132) ; other sources put the figure at 2 million.
13 Nodet and Taylor (1998, p. 288).
14 *Ibid.*, p. 289.
15 Norelli (2019, p. 85); Étienne Nodet and Justin Taylor believe that this phrase is more a reference to internal proselytism within Judaism.
16 Long (2012, pp. 50–57).
17 Mimouni (2017); Nodet and Taylor (1998, p. 32).
18 Liverani Mario (2007), p. 149.
19 Mazower Mark (2006, p. 18).
20 Schama (2013, p. 177).
21 Nodet and Taylor (1998, p. 287).
22 *Ibid.*, p. 291.
23 On the links between "pre-digital" social networks and innovation, see Rogers and Kincaid (1981).
24 Frankopan (2017 and 2018).
25 Dziembowski (2018).
26 Dumézil (2013, pp. 28–29).
27 Doan (2019).
28 Delumeau (1978), on fear in the West between the 14th and 18th centuries. In Congo, I discovered that 'witchcraft' is an anthropological i.e. universal mechanism to provide a conspiracy-based explanation for day-to-day misfortunes (Desjeux, 1987, pp. 178–205).

29 See Hervé Seitz (molecular biologist), "Covid-19 et chloroquine: mensonge et caprice à l'heure d'Internet 2.0", 26 March 2020 (www.youtube.com/watch?v=Bm-GJ4PF9ts). Quinine was also trialled in 1918, during the 'Spanish' flu, but had no effect, just like today (Spinney, 2017, pp. 110–111).
30 Taleb (2012).
31 Mimouni (2012, p. 15).
32 Kaplan (2016).
33 Cazelles and Grelot (1959, p. 90).

Chapter 5
The incremental invention launched by Jesus: purifying the Temple religion

1 Long (2012, p. 19).
2 Golb (1996, p. 40).
3 *Ibid.*, p. 73.
4 Bailly (c. 1960).
5 Long (2012, p. 19).
6 On schools of thought in Greece and the practice of philosophy in a relaxed form, see Pierre Vesperini (2019). He also recalls that the term *theory* (θεωρία) in ancient Greek does not have the abstract meaning that it has today, but that it means to see, to observe (p. 88).
7 Long (2012, location 6597).
8 *Encyclopédie* by Diderot (1765), "Sadducéen".
9 Collective (1956, p. 200, note a).
10 I discovered a case of 'levirate' in Congo when looking at the genealogy of a Sundi family in the 1970s, showing that it is not restricted to the Jewish tradition. The goal of this practice appears to be the same, namely to keep farmland within the maternal line of the Sundi family (Desjeux, 1987). Originally, Jewish kinship was patrilineal: "The Babylonian Talmud [sixth century AD] contains a terse summary of this situation: "it is the father's family that is called one's family, while one's mother's family is not called one's family." [b., Bava Batra 109b]" (Joseph Mélèze, 2009, "Père ou mère? Aux origines de la matrilinéarité juive", Clio.fr, 2009, p. 1).
11 Nodet and Taylor (1998, pp. 123).
12 See the core demonstration of Clayton M. Christensen (2000) showing that information technology innovations did not emerge within large companies but rather in small, marginal ones. See also Serge Moscovici (1979) on innovations produced by active minorities and conflicts.
13 Nodet (2009, p. 110).
14 Long (2011, p. 169 et seq.).
15 Golb (1996, p. 20).

Notes

16 Nodet and Taylor (1998, p. 124).
17 Nodet (2009, p. 82).
18 Douglas (1971).
19 Sfar (2018, p. 7).
20 See D. Desjeux (ed.), *Sur les innovations de réception*, to be published by PUF as an open book for online consultation (2022): www.puf.com.
21 See https://gbrisepierre.fr/article-presse/les-cles-de-la-transition-transfereurs-2021.
22 Long (2012, p. 26).
23 Nodet and Taylor (1998, pp. 159 and 443).
24 *Ibid.*, p. 153.
25 *Ibid.*, p. 195. Étienne Nodet is also a specialist in Flavius Josephus, who was a first-century-AD Judeo-Roman historian. Flavius Josephus, son of Mattias, evoked the historical existence of Jesus when he referred to "the brother of Jesus, who was called Christ, whose name was James" [Aslan, 2014, p. 23; from the text of Flavius Josephus, *Antiquities of the Jews*, XX, ix, 1, § 200, the source of which is cited by Paul-Hubert Poirier (2000, p. 532)].
26 *Ibid.*, p. 159.
27 *Ibid.*, pp. 155–156.
28 Long (2011, pp. 237–238).
29 Bernheim (1996/2003, pp. 154–155).
30 Long (2012, p. 27).
31 Long (2012, p. 22).
32 Nodet (2009).
33 Bultmann (1968).
34 Taponier and Desjeux Dominique (1994, pp. 240–243). The term "mobilizing figure" is inspired by the work of Haroun Jamous on decision (1969), which uses the term "reforming figure".
35 Long (2012, p. 23).
36 Mimouni, cited by Long (2012, p. 41).
37 Aslan (2013, chapter 12).
38 *Ibid.*, pp. 217–218.
39 See Cochoy (2002) on packaging.
40 On brands that are "as old as Cleopatra" or "as Herod", see Heilbrunn (2011).
41 Marguerat (1999, p. 203).
42 See C. Desjeux and B. Desjeux (2014).
43 Golb (1996, chapter 3).
44 Graeber (2015); Scott (2019); Clastres (1974); Sahlins (1976).
45 His last posthumous book, written with the archaeologist David Wengrow, advocates a completely different approach from the one I had previously understood, neither Rousseauist nor Hobbesian, which is much more interesting: David Graeber, David Wengrow (2021).
46 See Mathieu's (2022) book, *Comment la pensée logistique gouverne le monde*, which contains a fascinating global history of logistics. He ends by making it an essential

property specific to capitalism and its global domination, which seems less obvious. I wonder how yesterday's logistics would have been any less related to the social forces that dominated the Egyptian, Greek or Roman world. Like any structural social phenomenon, logistics and the energy related to it are ambivalent. They are sources of both liberation and domination.

47 See Mimouni (2012) for the transition from priests to rabbis; Mimouni and Pouderon (2012) for the separation of Church and Synagogue.
48 Long (2012, location 6456).

Chapter 6

Paul the Apostle on the road to disruptive innovation

1 Geoltrain (2000, p. xviii).
2 Arnould-Béhar (2007, location 324).
3 *Ibid.*, location 371.
4 *Ibid.*, locations 383 and 393.
5 Norelli (2019, p. 32).
6 Geoltrain (2000, p. xxv).
7 Jamous (1969).
8 Taponier and Desjeux (1994).
9 Marguerat (1999, p. 75).
10 Geoltrain (2000, p. xxvii).
11 *Ibid.*, p. 277.
12 Bronner (2021, p. 279).
13 Maraval and Mimouni (2006, location 8842).
14 Jerphagnon (2007).
15 Marguerat (1999, p. 227).
16 *Ibid.*, p. 236.
17 Norelli (2019); Geoltrain (2000); Marguerat (1999).
18 Nodet and Taylor (1998, p. 235, note 84).
19 Bernheim (1996/2003); Norelli (2019, p. 63).
20 Bernheim (1996/2003, pp. 286 and 290).
21 *Ibid.*, p. 340; Badiou (1997).
22 Maraval and Mimouni (2006, location 10632).
23 Reinhardt (2020).
24 Norelli (2019, p. 197 et seq.).
25 *Ibid.*, p. 202.
26 Long (2012, p. 152).

Notes

27 Bailly (c. 1960).
28 Festinger, Riecken and Schachter (1956/1993, p. 135).
29 Akrich, Callon and Latour (1988).
30 Festinger, Riecken and Schachter (1956/1993, chapter 1).
31 *Ibid.*, chapter 7.
32 Lisa Lerer, "Trump's Shadow Lingers Over Divided G.O.P.", *The New York Times*, 30 January 2021, (poll of 25 January 2021, Monmouth University).
33 Mathew Rosenberg, Jim Rutenberg, "Key Takeways From Trump's Effort to Overturn the Election", *The New York Times*, 1st February 2021.
34 Rand (2017, chapter 7).
35 Stella Cooper, Ben Decker, Anjali Singhvi, Christian Triebert, "Tracking the Oath Keepers Who Attacked the Capitol", *The New York Times*, 29 January 2021.
36 Adam Goldman, Katie Benner, Zolan Kanno-Youngs, "How Trump's Focus on Antifa Distracted Attention From the Far-Right Threat", *The New York Times*, 30 January 2021.
37 Stella Cooper, Ben Decker, Anjali Singhvi, Christian Triebert, "Tracking the Oath Keepers Who Attacked the Capitol", *The New York Times*, 29 January 2021.
38 "The American Abyss", *The New York Times*, 9 January 2021 by Timothy Snyder, a historian of US fascism.
39 See Andrew L. Whitehead and Samuel L. Perry, *Taking America Back for God. Christian Nationalism in the United States*, Oxford, Oxford University Press, 2020; Thomas B. Edsall, "The Capitol insurrection was as Christian nationalist as it gets. Religious resentment has become a potent recruiting tool for the hard right", *The New York Times*, 28 January 2021.
40 Morin (1969); Kapferer (1987); Campion-Vincent and Renard (2002); Campion-Vincent (2002 and 2005); Renard (1999).
41 Desjeux (1987 and 2018a).
42 Jauss (1990).
43 Sand (2009, p. 182).
44 *Idem.*
45 See Gadja (2002) on monotheism in southern Arabia.
46 See Althabe (1969) on Tromba, a Malagasy possession cult (practised by the Betsimisaraka on the east coast of the island).

Chapter 7

The destruction of the Temple: the incremental invention becomes a disruptive innovation

1. Schwentzel (2021).
2. Bettini (2023).
3. Schmitt Pantel (2015).
4. Golb (1996).
5. Norelli (2019, p. 185).
6. Taleb (2012).
7. Piatelli-Palmarini (1995, p. 39).
8. Camus (1961), in which the epigraph is taken from the Greek poet Pindar (fifth century BC): "O my soul, do not aspire to immortal life, but exhaust the limits of the possible."
9. Maraval and Mimouni (2006, location 5294).
10. Mimouni and Pouderon (2012, p. 15).
11. Mimouni (2012, p. 483).
12. Marek Halter includes the story of Yohanan ben Zakkai in his historical novel, *The Book of Abraham* (1986, p. 8).
13. Simon Claude Mimouni (2012).
14. Mimouni (2012, p. 484).
15. *Ibid.*, p. 486.
16. See Schmitt Pantel (2015, chapter 11) on the myth of Prometheus and the description of honouring Zeus through animal sacrifices, by fire, with bones and fat.
17. Mimouni (2012, p. 486).
18. Nodet (2009).
19. Mimouni (2012, p. 487).
20. Geoltrain (2000, p. xlvii).
21. As Gérald Bronner recalls in his book *Apocalypse cognitive* (2021, p. 190), before it acquired the meaning of catastrophe, *apocalypse* meant revelation: "disclosing a previously hidden truth" (Ἀποκάλυψις, the action of uncovering in ancient Greek).
22. Geoltrain (2000, p. xlv).
23. Marguerat (1999).
24. Geoltrain (2000, p. xlv).
25. Norelli (2019, p. 173).
26. Desjeux (1987).
27. Geoltrain (2000, p. xlv).
28. Maraval and Mimouni (2006, location 6743).
29. Schmitt Pantel (2015, chapter 11).
30. Norelli (2019, p. 166).
31. Long (2012, p. 19).

Chapter 8

The struggle between rabbinic Judaism and Christianity for control of the synagogues

1. Bronner (2021, p. 268).
2. Maraval and Mimouni (2006, location 9046).
3. Mimouni (2012, p. 482).
4. JPS Tanakh (1985, online: https://www.sefaria.org/texts/Tanakh).
5. Long (2012, p. 278): "God sent forth His Son, born of a *woman*, born under the law" (Gal. 4:4).
6. Maraval and Mimouni (2006, emplacement 11934).
7. Schmitt Pantel (2015, chapter 24).
8. Piclin (1993, p. 2288).
9. *Ibid.*, p. 2295.
10. Maraval and Mimouni (2006, location 9016).
11. Lenoir (2012, p. 92).
12. See Maraval and Mimouni (2006, locations 12644–12656).
13. *Ibid.*, location 5088.
14. Gugenheim (1992, p. 80).
15. Golb (1996).
16. Maraval and Mimouni (2006, location 5294).
17. Étienne Nodet and Justin Taylor note that the existence of synagogues prior to the third century AD is difficult to confirm (1998, p. 446). Whatever name we give them, places existed for Jews to meet and to pray, which we call synagogues, as in the Acts of the Apostles (17:1).
18. Nodet (2020, location 4491).
19. Geoltrain (2000, p. XLII).
20. Maraval and Mimouni (2006, location 4676).
21. *Ibid.*, location 4339.
22. *Ibid.*, location 5214.
23. Desjeux (1973).
24. Mimouni (2012, pp. 490 and 530).
25. Maraval and Mimouni (2006, location 5247).
26. *Ibid.*, location 5238.
27. Maraval and Mimouni (2006, location 13423).
28. *Ibid.*, location 13611.
29. Lenoir (2012, p. 97).
30. Maraval and Mimouni (2006, location 10077).
31. Lenoir (2012, p. 96).

32 Mimouni (2012, p. 490).
33 Brown (2012, chapter 1).
34 *Ibid.*, chapter 4.

Chapter 9

How the instability of the Roman Empire favoured the Christian innovation

1 Bettini (forthcoming 2023, p. 105).
2 Lamine (2004).
3 Piclin (1993, p. 2291).
4 Hadromi-Allouche (2017, p. 193).
5 Bettini (2023, p. 105).
6 *Ibid.*, p. 16.
7 Amzallag (2020, location 3325).
8 Bettini (2023, p. 106).
9 Schmitt Pantel (2015).
10 Bettini (2023, p. 106).
11 Hadromi-Allouche (2017, p. 193).
12 Bettini (2023, p. 93).
13 Pirenne-Delforge (2019, location 305).
14 See Drucker (1999). This article was given to me by my friend Mark Neumann when I was on assignment at USF (University of South Florida) in 1999.
15 Long (2012, p. 14).
16 Maraval and Mimouni (2006, location 4779).
17 Destro and Pesce (2012).
18 Geoltrain (2000, p. LIV).
19 Norelli (2019, p. 186).
20 Mordillat and Prieur (2008, pp. 147–148).
21 Norelli (2019, p. 186).
22 *Ibid.*, p. 413.
23 *Ibid.*, p. 185.
24 Geoltrain (2000, p. XLIX).
25 *Ibid.*, p. LI.
26 Maraval and Mimouni (2006, locations 12396, 12408 and 12431).
27 Lenoir (2012, pp. 136–139).
28 Maraval and Mimouni (2006, location 13983 et seq.).
29 Lenoir (2012, pp. 223 and 226–227).
30 *Ibid.*, p. 197.

Notes

31 Brown (2012, chapter 2).
32 *Ibid.*, chapter 2.
33 Norelli (2019, p. 180).
34 Costa (2012, p. 161).
35 Maraval and Mimouni (2006, location 9070).
36 For a summary of the debates in the book of Justin, see Long (2012, pp. 270–282).
37 Geoltrain (2000, p. XLIX).
38 *Ibid.*, p. XLIX.
39 Maraval and Mimouni (2006, location 9935).
40 *Ibid.*, location 9958.
41 *Ibid.*, location 10077.
42 *Ibid.*, location 10111.
43 *Ibid.*, location 14676 et seq.
44 Lenoir (2012, p. 217); Dumézil (2013b, p. 28).
45 Maraval and Mimouni (2006, location 10949).
46 *Ibid.*, locations 10940–11370; see Cuche (2019) on the cases of current diasporas and Mazower (2006) on those of historic diasporas.
47 Maraval and Mimouni (2006, location 11821).
48 *Ibid.*, location 11952.
49 *Ibid.*, locations 11673 and 11695.
50 *Ibid.*, location 14587.
51 Brown (2012, chapter 1, Harvest shocks).
52 Pomeranz (2010).
53 Dumézil (2013a and 2015). I discovered Bruno Dumézil thanks to my conversations on history and music with Mikael Mas, co-founder of the startup Symaps.
54 Veyne (2007).
55 Dumézil (2015).
56 Brown (2012, chapter 2).
57 *Ibid.*, chapter 2.
58 Dumézil (2015).
59 *Idem.*
60 *Idem.*
61 *Idem.*
62 Tarde (2001).
63 Jerphagnon (1986); Maraval (2015, location 2003 et seq.).
64 Brown (2000).
65 *Ibid.*
66 Cournault (2017).
67 MacMullen (1997, p. 71).
68 *Ibid.*, p. 14.
69 *Ibid.*, p. 17.

70 *Ibid.*, p. 58.
71 *Ibid.*, p. 22.
72 *Ibid.*, p. 157.
73 Nilsson (1955, p. 22) in French [Translator's note: this is a free translation from the French version]
74 Desjeux (1982, p. 108).

Conclusion

1 Dupont (2005, p. 17).
2 Collective (1998).
3 Brown (2000).
4 United States Conference of Catholic Bishops; see https://www.usccb.org/beliefs-and-teachings/what-we-believe. Emphasis by the author.
5 Father Robert Tamisier translated and annotated the Gospels of Mathew and Mark in 1978.
6 Desjeux (2018b).
7 Mauss (1950).
8 Desjeux (2021).
9 Mauss (1950).

Postscript

1 Desjeux (2018a, chapters 1 and 7).
2 Desjeux, Monjaret and Taponier (1998, p. 170 et seq.).
3 Benavent (2016); Moati (2011); Badot and Moreno (2017).
4 See Keck (2020).
5 Harper (2019, location 726); on scales of observation, see Desjeux (2018*a*, chapter 7; 2021); on energy in history, see Smil (1994).
6 Taponier and Desjeux (1994, chapter vi).
7 See https://consommations-et-societes.fr.
8 On lockdown viewed from inside the home, see Ankri (2020).
9 Desjeux and Clochard (2001).
10 Alter (2002); Gaglio (2011); Mustar and Penan (2003); Le Masson, Weil and Hatchuel (2006).
11 Akrich, Callon and Latour (1988); Edgerton (2013); Parker (1993); Caron (2010).
12 Crozier and Friedberg (1977).
13 Latour and Woolgar (1988); Pestre (2014).
14 Callon (2017); Diasio and Julien (2019).
15 Desjeux, Alami and Taponier (1998, pp. 75–88).
16 C. Desjeux and D. Desjeux (2020).

Notes

17 Desjeux, Monjaret and Taponier (1998, chapter VIII).
18 Warnier (1994); Julien and Rosselin (2005).
19 See www.youtube.com/watch?v=x2Y6WfPFnx-Q&ab_channel=Alcor-Media.
20 Bloch and Morin-Delerm (2011).
21 Harper (2019, location 8258 et seq.).

Bibliography

Akrich Madeleine, Callon Michel, Latour Bruno (1988), "À quoi tient le succès des innovations? L'art de l'intéressement", *Annales des Mines*.

Alter Norbert (2000), *L'Innovation ordinaire*, Paris, Puf.

Alter Norbert (dir.) (2002), *Les Logiques de l'innovation. Approche pluridisciplinaire*, Paris, La Découverte.

Althabe Gérard (1969), *Oppression et libération dans l'imaginaire. Les communautés villageoises de la côte orientale de Madagascar*, Paris, Maspero, preface by Georges Balandier.

Amzallag Nissim (2020), *La Forge de Dieu. Aux origines de la Bible*, Paris, Cerf (digital edition).

Angel Pierre, Bloch Alain, Coville Thierry, Marteau Fanny (2011), "Réflexions sur la décision entrepreneuriale", in Bloch Alain, Morin-Delerm Sophie (dir.), *Innovation et création d'entreprise. De l'idée à l'organisation*, Paris, ESKA, pp. 147–159.

Ankri Mazal (2020), *Je vous écris de Paris. 55 billets de confinement*, Paris, L'Harmattan.

Arnould-Béhar Caroline (2007), *La Palestine à l'époque romaine*, Paris, Les Belles Lettres (digital edition).

Aslan Reza (2013), *Zealot. The Life and Times of Jesus of Nazareth*, Random House.

Augé Marc (1982), *Génie du paganisme*, Paris, Gallimard.

Badiou Alain (1997), *Saint Paul. La fondation de l'universalisme*, Paris, Puf.

Badot Olivier, Moreno Dominique (2017), *Commerce et urbanisme commercial. Les grands enjeux de demain*, Caen, EMS Éditions.

Bailly Anatole (v. 1960), *Dictionnaire grec-français*, Paris, Hachette [1895].

Balandier Georges (1955), *Sociologie actuelle de l'Afrique noire. Dynamique des changements sociaux en Afrique centrale*, Paris, Puf.

Barnavi Élie (2002), *Histoire universelle des Juifs*, Paris, Hachette, "Littératures" (updated by Denis Charbit, first edition 1992).

BAUER Martin W. (2017), "Resistance as a latent factor of innovation", in GODIN Benoît, VINCK Dominique (dir.), *Critical Studies of Innovation*, Cheltenham, Edward Elgar Publishing, pp. 159–181.

BAYARD Pierre (2000), *Who Killed Roger Ackroyd?*, The New Press.

BENAVENT Christophe (2016), *Plateformes. Sites collaboratifs, marketplaces, réseaux sociaux… Comment ils influencent nos choix*, Limoges, FYP.

BENGTSSON Frans G. (1954), *The Long Ships: A Saga of the Viking Age*, Harper Collins Publishers (Kindle Edition).

BERNHEIM Pierre-Antoine (1996), *Jacques, frère de Jésus*, Paris, Albin Michel (2003 edition).

BETTINI Maurizio (2023), *In Praise of Polytheism*, University of California Press (translated by Douglas Grant Heise).

BLOCH Alain, MORIN-DELERM Sophie (dir.) (2011), *Innovation et création d'entreprise. De l'idée à l'organisation*, Paris, ESKA.

BOILEAU-NARCEJAC (1964), *Le Roman policier*, Paris, Petite Bibliothèque Payot.

BOISSIÈRE Yann (2020), "Les fondamentaux du judaïsme. Histoire juive 1 (cours 1/3)"; on YouTube: http://bit.ly/boissierefondamentauxjudaisme.

BOLTANSKI Luc, THÉVENOT Laurent (1991), *De la justification. Les économies de la grandeur*, Paris, Gallimard.

BOTTÉRO Jean (1992), *Naissance de Dieu. Le Bible et l'historien*, Paris, Gallimard, "Folio histoire" [1986].

BRONNER Gérald (2021), *Apocalypse cognitive*, Paris, Puf.

BROWN Peter (2000), *Augustine of Hippo, A Biography*, University of California Press.

——— (2012), *Through the Eye of a Needle: Wealth, the Fall of Rome, and the Making of Christianity in the West, 350–550 AD*, Princeton University Press

BULTMANN Rudolf (1968), *Jésus, mythologie et démythologisation*, Paris, Seuil [1926].

CALLON Michel (dir.) (1989), *La Science et ses réseaux. Genèse et circulation des faits scientifiques*, Paris, La Découverte.

——— (2017), *L'Emprise des marchés. Comprendre leur fonctionnement pour pouvoir les changer*, Paris, La Découverte.

CALLON Michel, LATOUR Bruno (1991), *La Science telle qu'elle se fait*, Paris, La Découverte.

CAMPION-VINCENT Véronique (2002), *De source sûre. Nouvelles rumeurs d'aujourd'hui*, Paris, Petite Bibliothèque Payot.

—— (2005), *La Société parano. Théories du complot, menaces et incertitudes*, Paris, Payot.

CAMPION-VINCENT Véronique, RENARD Jean-Bruno (1992), *Légendes urbaines. Rumeurs d'aujourd'hui*, Paris, Petite Bibliothèque Payot.

CAMUS Albert (2008), *The Myth of Sisyphus and Other Essays*, Paw Prints [1942].

CARON François (2010), *La Dynamique de l'innovation. Changement technique et changement social (xvie-xxe siècle)*, Paris, Gallimard.

CAZELLES Henri, GRELOT Pierre (1959), "Le texte de la Bible", in *Collectif, Introduction à la Bible*, Paris, Desclée et Cie, vol. Long (1, pp. 73–120).

CENTRE DE SOCIOLOGIE DE L'INNOVATION (1992), *Ces réseaux que la raison ignore*, Paris, L'Harmattan.

CHAVARIN Olivier (2017), "Symbole de Nicée Constantinople, traduction et commentaire"; online: https://testimonia.fr/symbole-de-nicee-constantinople-traduction-et-commentaire/.

CHRISTENSEN Clayton M. (2000), *The Innovator's Dilemma*, Boston, Harper Business.

CHRISTENSEN Clayton M., OVERDORF Michael (2003), "Répondre au défi du changement radical", in COLLECTIF, *Les Meilleurs Articles de la Harvard Business Review sur l'innovation*, Paris, Éditions d'organisation, pp. 127–157.

CLASTRES Pierre (1974), *La Société contre l'État. Recherche d'anthropologie politique*, Paris, Minuit.

CLÉVENOT Michel (1976), *Approche matérialiste de la Bible*, Paris, Cerf.

CLINE Eric H. (2016), *1177 avant J.-C. Le jour où la civilisation s'est effondrée*, Paris, La Découverte [2014].

COCHOY Franck (2002), *Une sociologie du packaging, ou l'âne de Buridan face au marché. Les emballages et le choix du consommateur*, Paris, Puf.

COLLECTIVE (1956), *La Sainte Bible. École biblique de Jérusalem*, Paris, Cerf.

COLLECTIVE (1998), *Pentateuque*, French translation under the direction of chief rabbi Zadoc Kahn, Jerusalem, Éditions Salomon.

Costa José (2012), "Le marqueur identitaire de la circoncision chez les rabbins de l'Antiquité", in Mimouni Simon Claude, Pouderon Bernard (dir.), *La Croisée des chemins revisités*, Paris, Cerf, pp. 161–194.

Cournault Philippe (2017), "*La Cité de Dieu* de saint Augustin: une histoire identitaire en réponse à un trouble politique?", *Essais. Revue interdisciplinaire d'humanités*, n° 11, pp. 17–28.

Crozier Michel, Friedberg Erhard (1977), *L'Acteur et le Système*, Paris, Seuil.

Cuche Denys (2019), *Les Palestiniens chrétiens du Pérou. Anthropologie d'une diaspora de chrétiens orientaux*, Paris, L'Harmattan.

Delumeau Jean (1978), *La Peur en Occident: une cité assiégée (XIV-XVIIe siècle)*, Paris, Fayard.

Desjeux Catherine, Desjeux Bernard (2014), *Vodun et Orisha. La voix des dieux*, Brinon-sur-Sauldre, Grandvaux.

Desjeux Cyril, Desjeux Dominique (2020), "Handicap et consommation: pour une épistémologie inclusive des recherches de terrain"; en ligne: https://consommations-et-societes.fr/2021-01-cyril-desjeux-sociologue-dominique-desjeux-anthropologue-handicap-et-consommation-pour-une-epistemologie-inclusive-des-recherches-de-terrain/

Desjeux Dominique (1971–1975), "La culture du riz à Madagascar", video.

——— (1973), *Le Corps des Mines: un nouveau mode d'intervention de l'État*, masters thesis under the direction of Michel Crozier (Paris X), Paris, Microéditions Hachette [1971].

——— (1979), *La Question agraire à Madagascar. Administration et paysannat de 1895 à nos jours*, Paris, L'Harmattan.

——— (1982), "L'Afrique musulmane", *Le Mois en Afrique*, mai-juin, pp. 102–109.

——— (1984), *L'Eau. Quels enjeux pour les sociétés rurales?*, Paris, L'Harmattan.

——— (1987), *Strategie paysanne en Afrique noire. Le Congo. Essai sur la gestion de l'incertitude*, Paris, L'Harmattan.

——— (1991), *Le Sens de l'autre*, UNESCO/L'Harmattan.

——— (2013), "Le marketing entre cadrage, consommateurs acteurs et nouvelles émergence sociétale", in Bourgne Patrick (dir.), *Marketing: remède ou poison? Les effets du marketing dans une société en crise*, Caen, EMS Éditions,- 95/-115, 17.

——— (2018a), *L'Empreinte anthropologique du monde. Méthode inductive illustrée*, Bruxelles, Peter Lang.

——— (2018b), "Bronislaw Malinowski, or the elementary material and symbolic forms of production, exchange and consumption", in Askegaard Soren, Heilbrunn Benoît (eds.), *Canonical Authors in Consumption Theory*, Londres, Routledge.

——— (2021), *Scales of Observation*, Oxford Research Encyclopedias, published online: 22 December 2021 https://consommations-et-societes.fr/2022-01-scales-of-observation-dominique-desjeux/

Desjeux Dominique, Alami Sophie, Taponier Sophie (1998), "Les pratiques d'organisation du travail domestique: 'une structure d'attente spécifique'", in Bonnet Michel, Bernard Yvonne (dir.), *Services de proximité et vie quotidienne*, Paris, Puf.

Desjeux Dominique, Berthier Cécile, Jarraffoux Sophie, Orhant Isabelle, Taponier Sophie (1996), *Anthropologie de l'électricité. Les objets électriques dans la vie quotidienne en France*, Paris, L'Harmattan.

Desjeux Dominique, Clochard Fabrice (2001), "La vente à distance (VAD)"; on line: https://consommations-et-societes.fr/2001-d-desjeux-f-clochard-la-vente-a-distance-vad/.

Desjeux Dominique, Monjaret Anne, Taponier Sophie (1998), *Quand les Français déménagent. Circulation des objets domestiques et rituels de mobilité dans la vie quotidienne en France*, Paris, Puf.

Desjeux Dominique, Sarah Charlotte (2020), "Les effets du confinement sur les comportements alimentaires des Français pendant la crise du Covid-19", online executive summary: https://consommations-et-societes.fr/wp-content/uploads/2020/07/2020-07-PWT-SYN-THESE-5-FRANCAIS.pdf.

Desjeux Dominique, Yang Xiaomin (2017), "L'observation de l'émergence de la classe moyenne chinoise à partir de 1997 (les photos et les objets familiaux comme trace matérielle de la mémoire)", in Yang Xiaomin, Zheng Lihua (dir.), *Chine-France: connaître et reconnaître*, Paris, Le Manuscrit.

Destro Andriana, Pesce Mauro (2012), "From Jesus movement to christianity", in Mimouni Simon Claude, Pouderon Bernard (dir.), *La Croisée des chemins revisitée*, Paris, Cerf, pp. 21–49.

Diasio Nicoletta, Julien Marie-Pierre (dir.) (2019), *Anthropology of Family Food Practices. Constraints, Adjustments, Innovations*, Berne, Peter Lang.

Doan Raphaël (2019), *Quand Rome inventait le populisme*, Paris, Cerf.

Dogan Mattei, Pahre Robert (1991), *L'Innovation dans les sciences sociales. La marginalité créatrice*, Paris, Puf.

Douglas Mary (1971), *De la souillure. Essai sur les notions de tabou et de pollution*, Paris, Maspero/La Decouverte.

Drucker Peter (1999), "Beyond the information revolution", *Atlantic Monthly*, October.

Dumézil Bruno (2010), *Les Royaumes barbares en Occident*, Paris, Puf, « Que sais-je? ».

——— (2013a), *Des Gaulois aux Carolingiens, Une histoire de France*, Paris, Puf.

——— (2013b), *Servir l'État barbare dans la Gaule franque. Du fonctionnariat antique à la noblesse médiévale (ive-ixe siècle)*, Paris, Tallandier.

——— (2015), "Les invasions barbares", conference of 21 March; online on YouTube: http://bit.ly/Dumezilinvasionbarbares.

Dupont Florence (2005), *Homère et Dallas*, Paris, Kimé.

Dziembowski Edmond (2018), *La Guerre de Sept Ans*, Paris, Perrin.

Edgerton David (2013), *Quoi de neuf? Du rôle des techniques dans l'histoire globale*, Paris, Seuil [2008].

Fagan Brian (2017), *La Grande Histoire de ce que nous devons aux animaux*, Paris, Vuibert.

Febvre Lucien (1942), *Le Problème de l'incroyance au xvie siècle. La religion de Rabelais*, Paris, Albin Michel.

Festinger Leon, Riecken Henry, Schachter Stanley (2008), *When Prophecy Fails*, Pinter & Martin [first published in 1956].

Finkelstein Israël, Römer Thomas (2019), *Aux origines de la Torah*, Paris, Bayard.

Frankopan Peter (2017), *Les Routes de la soie*, Bruxelles, Nevicata [2015].

——— (2018), *Les Nouvelles Routes de la soie*, Bruxelles, Nevicata.

Gadja Iwona (2002), "Les débuts du monothéisme en Arabie du Sud", *Journal asiatique*, 290, n. 2, pp. 611–630.

Gaglio Gérald (2011), *Sociologie de l'innovation*, Paris, Puf, "Que sais-je?".

Bibliography

—— (2017), "'Innovation fads' as an alternative research topic to pro-innovation bias: The examples of Jugaad and reverse innovation", in GODIN Benoît, VINCK Dominique (dir.), *Critical Studies of Innovation*, Cheltenham, Edward Elgar Publishing, pp. 33–47.

GEOLTRAIN Pierre (dir.) (2000), *Aux origines du christia nisme*, Paris, Gallimard, "Folio histoire".

GISEL Pierre, EMERY Gilles (dir.) (2001), *Le christianisme est-il un monothéisme?*, Labor et Fides.

GODIN Benoît, VINCK Dominique (dir.) (2017), *Critical Studies of Innovation*, Cheltenham, Edward Elgar Publishing.

GOLB Norman (1996), *Who Wrote the Dead Sea Scrolls? The Search for The Secret of Qumran*, Touchstone. Plon [1995].

GRAEBER David (2006), *Pour une anthropologie anarchiste*, Paris, Éditions Lux.

GRAEBER David (2015), *Bureaucratie*, Paris, Les Liens qui libèrent.

GRAEBER David, WENGROW David (2021), *Au commencement était… Une nouvelle histoire de l'humanité*, Paris, Les liens qui libèrent (édition numérique).

GUGENHEIM Ernest (1992), *Le Judaïsme dans la vie quotidienne*, Paris, Albin Michel [1961].

HADROMI-ALLOUCHE Zohar (2017), "Name him 'Abd al-Harith'. Eve's fall from monotheism and ascent into motherhood", in HADROMI-ALLOUCHE Zohar, LARKIN Áine (dir.), *Fall Narratives. An Interdisciplinary Perspective*, Londres, Routledge.

HALTER Marek (1985), *La Mémoire d'Abraham*, Paris, Presses Pocket, [1983].

HARPER Kyle (2017), *The Fate of Rome: Climate, Disease, and the End of an Empire*, Princeton University Press.

—— (2019), French translation by Philippe Pignarre, *Comment l'Empire romain s'est effondré. Le climat, les maladies et la chute de Rome*, Paris, La Découverte (preface by Benoît Rossignol, digital edition).

HEILBRUNN Benoît (2011), Adaptation française de CHIARAVALLE Bill, FINDLAY Schenck Barbara, *Les Marques pour les nuls*, Paris, First.

HORVILLEUR Delphine (2020), *Le Rabbin et le Psychanalyste*, Paris, Hermann.

HU Shen, DESJEUX Dominique (2014), "Les usages sociaux de l'alcool des Chinois en Chine, Taïwan et Singapour"; en ligne sur Vimeo: https://vimeo.com/428984541.

Jamous Haroun (1969), *Sociologie de la décision. La réforme des études médicales et des structures hospitalières*, Paris, CNRS.

Jauss Hans Robert (1990), *Pour une esthétique de la réception*, Paris, Gallimard.

Jerphagnon Lucien (2008), *Julien, dit l'Apostat*, Paris, Seuil (édition [2006]).

——— (2007), *Laudator temporis acti (c'était mieux avant)*, Paris, Tallandier.

Julien Marie-Pierre, Rosselin Céline (2005), *La Culture matérielle*, Paris, La Découverte.

Kapferer Jean-Noël (1987), *Rumeur. Le plus vieux média du monde*, Paris, Seuil.

Kaplan Michel (2016), *Pourquoi Byzance? Un empire de onze siècles*, Paris, Gallimard.

Keck Frédéric (2020), *Les Sentinelles des pandémies. Chasseur de virus et observateurs d'oiseaux aux frontières de la Chine*, Bruxelles, Zones sensibles, 2e éd.

Khosro Khazai (2007), *The Gathas: The Sublime Book of Zarathustra*, Brussels, European Centre for Zoroastrian Studies, (Kindle Edition).

Laffon Martine (2009), *Gilgamesh*, adapted from the French translation by Jean Bottéro, Paris, Belin.

Lamine Anne-Sophie (2004), *La Cohabitation des dieux. Pluralité religieuse et laïcité*, Paris, Puf.

Latour Bruno (2011), *Pasteur: guerre et paix des microbes*, Paris, La Découverte [1984].

Latour Bruno, Woolgar Steve (1988), *La Vie de laboratoire. La production des faits scientifiques*, Paris, La Découverte [1979].

Le Masson Pascal, Weil Benoît, Hatchuel Armand (2006), *Les Processus d'innovation. Conception innovante et croissance des entreprises*, Cachan, Lavoisier.

Lemire Vincent (dir.) (2016), *Jérusalem. Histoire d'une ville-monde des origines à nos jours*, Paris, Flammarion, "Champs histoire" (digital edition).

Lenoir Frédéric (2012), *Comment Jésus est devenu Dieu*, Paris, Fayard [2010].

Liverani Mario (2007), *Israel's History and the History of Israel*, Equinox [2003].

Bibliography

LONG Didier (2011), *Jésus de Nazareth, juif de Galilée*, Paris, Presses de la Renaissance.

——— (2012), *L'Invention du christianisme*, Paris, Presse de la Renaissance (with e-book references).

MACMULLEN Ramsay (1997), *Christianity and Paganism in the Fourth to Eighth Centuries*, New Haven, Yale University Press.

MARAVAL Pierre (2015), *Le Christianisme de Constantin à la conquête arabe*, Paris, Puf. (des références e-book).

MARAVAL Pierre, MIMOUNI Simon Claude (2006), *Le Christianisme, des origines à Constantin*, Paris, Puf (e-book references).

MARGUERAT Daniel (1999), *La Première Histoire du christianisme. Les Actes des apôtres*, Paris, Cerf.

MARKS Robert B. (2007), *The Origins of the Modern World. A Global and Ecological Narrative*, Lanham, Rowman & Littlefield [2001].

MARTINEZ-GROS Gabriel (2021), *De l'autre côté des croisades. L'Islam entre croisés et Mongols*, Paris, Passé Composé (e-book references).

MAUSS Marcel (1950), *Sociologie et anthropologie*, Paris, Puf.

MAZOWER Mark (2006), *Salonica, City of Ghost. Christians, Muslims and Jews. 1430-1950*, New York, Vintage Books.

MIMOUNI Simon Claude (2004), *Les Chrétiens d'origine juive dans l'Antiquité*, Paris, Albin Michel.

——— (2007), *La Circoncision dans le monde judéen aux époques grecque et romaine. Histoire d'un conflit interne au judaïsme*, Louvain, Peeters.

——— (2012), *Le Judaïsme ancien du vie siècle avant notre ère au iiie siècle de notre ère. Des prêtres aux rabbins*, Paris, Puf.

——— (2017), "Origines du christianisme", conférence à l'EPHE; online: https://journals.openedition.org/asr/1598.

——— (2019), *Introduction à l'histoire des origines du christianisme*, Paris, Bayard.

MIMOUNI Simon Claude, POUDERON Bernard (dir.) (2012), *La Croisée des chemins revisitée. Quand l'Église et la Synagogue se sont-elles distinguées?*, Paris, Cerf.

MOATI Philippe (2011), *La Nouvelle Révolution commerciale*, Paris, Odile Jacob.

Mordillat Gérard, Prieur Jérôme (2008), *Jésus sans Jésus, la christianisation de l'Empire romain*, Paris, Seuil.

Morin Edgar (1969), *La Rumeur d'Orléans*, Paris, Seuil.

Moscovici Serge (1979), *Psychologie des minorités actives*, Paris, Puf.

Mustar Philippe, Penan Hervé (dir.) (2003), *Encyclopédie de l'innovation*, Paris, Economica.

Nilsson Martin P. (1955), *Les croyances religieuse de la Grèce Antique*, Payot [Translator's note: possibly Nilsson Martin P. (1948), *Greek Piety*, Clarendon Press].

—— (1964). *A History of Greek Religion*, Oxford at the Clarendon Press.

Nodet Étienne (2009), "Le baptême des prosélytes, rite d'origine essénienne", *Revue biblique*, 116, n° 1, pp. 82–110; online: www.jstor.org/stable/44090923.

—— (2020), "Postface", in Amzallag Nissim (dir), *La Forge de Dieu. Aux origines de la Bible*, Paris, Cerf (digital edition).

Nodet Étienne, Taylor Justin (1998), *The Origins of Christianity. An Exploration*, The Liturgical Press.

Norelli Enrico (2019), *La Naissance du christianisme. Comment tout a commencé*, Paris, Gallimard, « Folio histoire » [2014].

Parker Geoffray (1993), *La Révolution militaire. La guerre et l'essor de l'Occident 1500–1800*, Paris, Gallimard.

Pedrola Adèle, Potard Céline (2018), *Les Plus Beaux Récits de la mythologie grecque*, Paris, Philippe Auzou.

Pestre Dominique (dir.) (2014), *Le Gouvernement des technosciences. Gouverner le progrès et ses dégâts depuis 1945*, Paris, La Découverte.

Piatelli Palmarini Massimo (1995), *La Réforme du jugement ou Comment ne plus se tromper*, Paris, Odile Jacob [1993].

Piclin Michel (1993), "Plotin et le plotinisme", *Dictionnaire des philosophes*, Paris, Puf, pp. 228–229.

Pierron Bénédicte, Desjeux Dominique (2017), "La pratique du selfie, ou les jeux identitaires du Je"; en ligne: https://2015-2018.ludocorpus.org/wp-content/uploads/2017/05/2017-04-SELFIE-JEU-JE-V12.pdf

Pirenne-Delforge Vinciane (2019), *Le Polythéisme grec comme objet d'histoire*, Paris, Collège de France (des références e-book).

Bibliography

POIRIER Paul-Hubert (2000), "Jacques, frère de Jésus, dans trois livres récents" *Esthétique et philosophie*, vol. Long 3, pp. 531–541.

POMERANZ Kenneth (2010), *Une grande divergence. La Chine, l'Europe et la construction de l'économie mondiale*, Paris, Albin Michel.

PRIEUR Jérôme, MORDILLAT Gérard (2004a), *Corpus Christi. Enquête sur une énigme nommée Jésus*, Arte, série documentaire de douze épisodes.

——— (2004b), *Jésus après Jésus. L'origine du christianisme*, Paris, Seuil.

RAKOTO RAMIARANTSOA Hervé (1995), *Chair de la terre, œil de l'eau. Paysanneries et recompositions de campagnes en Imerina (Madagascar)*, Montpellier, IRD Éditions.

RAND Ayn (1996), *Atlas Shrugged*, Signet [1957].

REINHARDT Éric (2020), *Comédies françaises*, Paris, Gallimard (version Kindle).

RENARD Jean-Bruno (1999), *Rumeurs et légendes urbaines*, Paris, Puf, "Que sais-je?".

ROCHER Guy (1968), *Le Changement social*, Paris, Seuil.

ROGERS Everett M., KINCAID D. Lawrence (1981), *Communication Networks. Toward a New Paradigm for Research*, New York, Free Press [1962].

SAHLINS Marshall (1976), *Âge de pierre, âge de l'abondance. L'économie des sociétés primitives*, Paris, Gallimard [1972].

SAND Shlomo (2009), *The Invention of the Jewish People*, Verso.

SCHAMA Simon (2013), *The Story of the Jews: Finding the Words 1000 BC – 1492 AD*, Ecco.

SCHMITT PANTEL Pauline (2015), *Histoire des mythes grecs*, Paris, Puf/ Frémeaux & Associés (audible, 4 CD).

SCHWENTZEL Christian-Georges (2021), "Cassandre, la prophétesse qui disait toujours la vérité", *The Conversation*, 4 mars.

SCOTT James C. (2019), Homo domesticus. *Une histoire profonde des premiers États*, Paris, La Découverte [2017].

SFAR Joann (2018), *Le Chat du rabbin*, vol. 8: *Petit panier aux amandes*, Paris, Dargaud.

SIMON-NAHUM Perrine (2008), "L'Orient d'Ernest Renan: de l'étude des langues à l'histoire des religions", *Revue germanique internationale*, n° 7, pp. 157–168; en ligne: https://journals.openedition.org/rgi/406.

SMIL Vaclav (1994), *Energy and Civilization*, Cambridge, MIT Press.

Soler Jean (2002), *L'Invention du monothéisme. Aux origines du Dieu unique*, Paris, Éditions de Fallois.

Spinney Laura (2017), *Pale Rider. The Spanish Flu of 1918 and How It Changed the World*, Penguin, Londres (édition numérique)

Sun Tzu (1988), *The Art of War*, Translated by Thomas Cleary, Boston, Shambhala Dragon Editions.

Taleb Nassim Nicholas (2012), *Le Cygne noir. La puissance de l'imprévisible*, Paris, Les Belles Lettres.

Taponier Sophie, Desjeux Dominique (1994), *Informatique, décision et marché de l'informatique en agriculture*, Paris, L'Harmattan.

Tarde Gabriel (2001), *Les Lois de l'imitation*, Paris, Les Empêcheurs de penser en rond [1895].

Tocqueville Alexis (de) (1964), *L'Ancien Régime et la Révolution*, Paris, Club français du livre [1856].

Trevisan Semi Emanuela (1999), "Universalisme juif et prosélytisme. L'action de Jacques Faitlovitch, 'père' des Beta Israel (Falashas)", *Revue de l'histoire des religions*, vol. Long 2, pp. 193–211.

Vesperini Pierre (2019), *La Philosophie antique. Essai d'histoire*, Paris, Fayard (version Kindle).

Veyne Paul (1976), *Le Pain et le Cirque. Sociologie historique d'un pluralisme politique*, Paris, Seuil.

―――― (2007), *Quand notre monde est devenu chrétien (312–314)*, Paris, Albin Michel.

Warnier Jean-Pierre (1994), *Construire la culture matérielle. L'homme qui pensait avec ses doigts*, Paris, Puf.

Will Édouard, Orrieux Claude (1992), *"Prosélytisme juif"? Histoire d'une erreur*, Paris, Les Belles Lettres.

Zoja Luigi (2018), *Paranoïa. La folie qui fait l'histoire*, Paris, Les Belles Lettres.

Titres parus

Vol. 36 – Dominique Desjeux, *The Market of the Gods. How religious innovations emerge. From Judaism to Christianity*, 2024.

Vol. 35 – Fedoua Kasmi, Mauricio Camargo, Laurent Dupont (dir.), *Territoires en transition et innovation. Enjeux et outils d'accompagnement*, 2024.

Vol. 34 – Hubert Bonin, *Les responsabilités de l'entreprise*, 2024.

Vol. 33 – Nathalie Dupont, Laetitia Garcia (dir.), *Tourisme, arts et territoires. Impacts réciproques à travers des études de cas*, 2024.

Vol. 32 – Elachhab Fathi, *Macroéconomie quantitative et théorie des fluctuations. Applications aux pays en développement*, 2024.

Vol. 31 – Laurent Adatto, Camille Aouinaït, Son Thi Kim Le and Michelle Mongo (Eds.), *Innovation Ecosystems in the New Economic Era. Digital Revolution and Ecological Transition*, 2023.

Vol. 30 – Joëlle Forest et Bertrand Bocquet (dir.), *Imaginer le futur à partir du passé*, 2023.

Vol. 29 – Manon Enjolras, Mauricio Camargo, Christophe Schmitt (eds.), *Innovation and Internationalization of Small and Medium Enterprises. A Crossroads Perspective*, 2022.

Vol. 28 – Samuel-Jacques Priso-Essawe, *Intégration régionale « appropriée » en Afrique. Éléments juridiques d'effectivité*, 2021.

Vol. 27 – Vincent Herbert (dir.), *Tourisme et Territoires. Espaces d' innovations*, 2021.

Vol. 26 – Jean-Alain Héraud et Nathalie Popiolek, *L'organisation et la valorisation de la recherche. Problématique européenne et étude comparée de la France et de l'Allemagne*, 2021.

Vol. 25 – Stéphanie Lachaud-Martin, Corinne Marache, Julie McIntyre, Mikaël Pierre (eds.), *Wine, Networks and Scales. Intermediation in the Production, Distribution and Consumption of Wine*, 2021.

Vol. 24 – Verónica González-Araujo, Roberto-Carlos Álvarez-Delgado, Ángel Sancho-Rodríguez (eds.), *Ethics in Business Communication. New Challenges in the Digital World*, 2020.

Vol. 23 – Didier Caveng, *L'éthique dans la finance. Les banques genevoises à l'épreuve des faits*, 2019.

Vol. 22 – André Tiran et Dimitri Uzunidis (dir.), *Libéralisme et protectionnisme*, 2019.

Vol. 21 – Dominique Desjeux, *The anthropological perspective of the world. The inductive method illustrated*, 2018.

Vol. 20 – Benoît Bernard, *Management Public. 65 schémas pour analyser et changer les organisations publiques*, 2018.

Vol. 19 – Dimitri Uzunidis (dir.), *Recherche académique et innovation. La force productive de la science*, 2018.

Vol. 18 – Jean Vercherand, *Le marché du travail. L'esprit libéral et la revanche du politique*, 2018.

Vol. 17 – Dominique Desjeux (dir.), *L'empreinte anthropologique du monde. Méthode inductive illustrée*, 2018.

Vol. 16 – Sophie Boutillier, *Entrepreneuriat et innovation*, 2017.

Vol. 15 – Arvind Ashta, *Microfinance. Battling a Wicked Problem*, 2016.

Vol. 14 – Jean Vercherand, *Microéconomie. Une approche critique : Théorie et exercices*, 2016.

Vol. 13 – Réseau de Recherche sur l'innovation, Blandine Laperche (dir.), *Géront' innovations. Trajectoires d'innovation dans une économie vieillissante*, 2016.

Vol. 12 – Société Internationale Jean-Baptiste Say, Dimitri Uzunidis (dir.), *Et Jean-Baptiste Say… créa l'Entrepreneur*, 2015.

Vol. 11 – Faïz Gallouj, Francois Stankiewicz (dir.), *Le DRH innovateur. Management des ressources humaines et dynamiques d'innovation*, 2014.

Vol. 10 – Charlotte Fourcroy, *Services et environnement. Les enjeux énergétiques de l'innovation dans les services*, 2014.

Vol. 9 – Rémy Herrera, Wim Dierckxsens, Paulo Nakatani (eds.), *Beyond the Systemic Crisis and Capital-Led Chaos. Theoretical and Applied Studies*, 2014.

Vol. 8 – Réseau de Recherche sur l'Innovation, Sophie Boutillier, Joëlle Forest, Delphine Gallaud, Blandine Laperche, Corinne Tanguy, Leïla Temri (dir.), *Principes d'économie de l'innovation*, 2014.

Vol. 7 – Michel Santi, *Capitalism without Conscience*, 2013.

Vol. 6 – Arnaud Diemer, Jean-Pierre Potier, Léon Walras, *Un siècle après (1910–2010)*, 2013.

Vol. 5 – Sophie Boutillier, Faridah Djellal, Dimitri Uzunidis (Réseau de Recherche sur l'Innovation) (dir.), *L'innovation. Analyser, anticiper, agir*, 2013.

Vol. 4 – Aurélie Trouvé, Marielle Berriet-Solliec, Denis Lépicier (dir.), *Le développement rural en Europe. Quel avenir pour le deuxième pilier de la Politique agricole commune ?*, 2013.

Vol. 3 – Sophie Boutillier, Faridah Djellal, Faïz Gallouj, Blandine Laperche, Dimitri Uzunidis (dir.), *L'innovation verte. De la théorie aux bonnes pratiques*, 2012.

Vol. 2 – Faridah Djellal, Faïz Gallouj, *La productivité à l'épreuve des services*, 2012.

Vol. 1 – Abdelillah Hamdouch, Sophie Reboud, Corinne Tanguy (dir.), *PME, dynamiques entrepreneuriales et innovation*, 2011.